TRACES OF ENAYAT

TRACES OF ENAYAT

Iman Mersal

Translated from the Arabic by
Robin Moger

**TRANSIT
BOOKS**

Published by Transit Books
1569 Solano Ave #142, Berkeley, CA 94707
www.transitbooks.org

ISBN: 978-1-945492-84-6 (paperback)
LIBRARY OF CONGRESS CONTROL NUMBER: 2023951580

COVER DESIGN
Anna Morrison

TYPESETTING
Justin Carder

Printed in the United States of America
9 8 7 6 5 4 3 2 1

TRACES OF ENAYAT

But Paula hadn't gone to the funeral. She didn't know where the grave was.

She repeated the story I'd heard from her before, the same details in the same order:

That after receiving the phone call she had gone to Astra Square in Dokki, to the apartment there, bounding up the stairs to the second floor.

That it had been true what she'd been told: they had broken down the bedroom door searching for her.

That she had seen her stretched out on the bed, beautiful, as though peacefully asleep, the blanket laid over her smooth and neat.

"She'd made up her mind and there was no going back, you see. Such determination! She wasn't playing around."

Then Paula had lost her mind, swearing at the sleeping woman and beating her hands against the walls. She had left the apartment. And hadn't gone to the funeral.

At eight in the morning, February 19, 2015, I commended myself to God and caught a taxi to Basateen. All I had to go on was an address that had run in *al-Ahram* back in January 1967: *In memory of the late Enayat al-Zayyat, with hearts full of patience and faith, the family is holding a service in her memory which shall not be forgotten, at the tomb of the late Rashid Pasha in al-Afifi.*

Something about these lines itched at me. Demanded I edit them. Say,

Notice in the deaths column of al-Ahram, January 1967

. . . *the family will hold a memorial service today for* she *who shall not be forgotten, at the tomb of the late Rashid Pasha, al-Afifi.*

Finding this little paragraph among the death notices, I had been sure that there must be more stories. Among the memories of those still living, say, or in books, or on the shelves of public archives. That all I needed to do was be patient. But now, years after I'd first chanced across this clipping, reverently preserving it as though it were Enayat's identity card, and following the series of telephone conversations with Paula the previous autumn, I still had no idea who Rashid Pasha was, nor anything about his relationship to Enayat. I didn't even know his first name.

Was he from an Egyptian family, or Turkish? Was he Circassian? Nothing.

One of those nineteenth-century pashas, was my guess: men who strutted about with their entourages, sauntering through the palaces and vast estates granted them during the reign of Mohammed Ali, and whose legacies were the mausoleums which bear their names.

I found four men from the period that might fit the bill:

The first was a Turkish diplomat by the name of Mustafa Rashid Pasha, born in Istanbul and buried there in 1858. Jurji Zaidan dedicates a chapter to him in *Lives of the Great Men of the Orient in the Nineteenth Century*.

Second was Rashid Pasha al-Kouzlaki, originally from Kyrgyzstan, who was appointed wali of Baghdad by the Ottoman sultan in 1853 after leading a military campaign to crush a Kurdish rebellion in northern Mesopotamia, only to be buried in Baghdad just four years later, in the al-Khayzuran cemetery behind the dome of Abu Hanifa al-Numan's mausoleum. It was just possible that one of his sons was buried in al-Afifi.

The third Rashid Pasha had an interesting story. A Circassian who spoke Arabic with an accent, he is mentioned in Ilyas al-Ayoubi's history of Khedive Ismail's military expedition against the Ethiopian Empire. Rashid Pasha went south on the steamship *Dakahlia* with the other commanders, reaching Massawa on December 14, 1875. Al-Ayoubi gives a description of an onboard Babel: the commander in chief of the campaign, Ratib Pasha, was Turkish; Maj. Gen. William Wing Loring, his chief of staff, was American; the rest of the officers were a mix of Turks, Circassians, Americans, Austrians, and Germans, along with one Italian convert to Islam and a Sudanese.

Al-Ayoubi claims that although they had little combat experience themselves, the Turks and Circassians, Ratib Pasha and Rashid Pasha among them, conspired to withhold their cooperation from Loring and frustrate his plans. The resulting confusion led to the overwhelming victory of Ethiopian forces at the Egyptian-held fort at Gura on March 7, 1876. Some 3,273 Egyptians were killed and 1,416 were wounded, with just 530 escaping the battle unscathed.

Rashid Pasha was killed in the fighting. According to al-Ayoubi, as he lay in his own blood, Ethiopian soldiers stripped his body of its finery, dividing the haul among themselves and castrating him, before moving off to pursue the rout—meaning that this Rashid was buried, if he was buried at all, in Ethiopia.

The dead were buried in the wadi and the streambeds, writes al-Ayoubi. *There were almost two thousand of them, and they were not interred properly, for the rains soon washed the topsoil from their corpses and the wild beasts fed on their flesh.*

Reading this, I was secretly hoping that this improbable Rashid would not turn out to be Enayat's.

The final Rashid Pasha came from a family with close ties to Mohammed Ali. His name first enters the record in the 1850s, on a list of officials responsible for digging canals, draining marshland, and reclaiming desert land for agriculture. By 1868 he was governor of Cairo. He was among the founders of the Egyptian Geographic Society in 1875, and a year later he joined what was then called the Privy Council, where he headed the precursor of the Ministry of Finance. From January 1878 to April 1879, he was Speaker of the final parliamentary sessions to be held in the reign of Khedive Ismail.

There is almost no information about his origins or life outside of these facts, though in 1868 we find him registered as a member of the Society of Knowledge, which places him, in the historian al-Rafai's words, *among the best classes in society*.

To take the tone of a policier: it looked like this was the Rashid Pasha I wanted. If he turned out to be the owner of the tomb where Enayat lay, I would have to return to his story, but first I needed to see the tomb for myself.

The driver took Salah Salem Street as far as Sayyida Aisha Square, where he turned right, dropping me off a few minutes later at a narrow opening in a wall that ran parallel to the road.

"Ask here," he said. "There's a thousand can show you the way."

I stepped through the opening onto a ruler-straight street. To my right there was a high wall broken by sections of black corrugated iron, and to my left the entrances to the tombs, each dressed in a fresh coat of yellow. I saw a little girl trotting towards me. She wore a violet robe flounced in tiers, loaves slumped across the lattice of palm fronds that she balanced on her head. The sight was so compelling that I longed to take a picture and wished I had a tourist's audacity.

The girl passed me, then the scrape of her sandals stopped abruptly and I looked round to find her standing and staring. Our eyes met. Did she know where al-Afifi was? "Man or street?" She was older than I'd thought. I took a couple of steps towards her and asked the way to the nearest bakery. She described it precisely.

It wasn't as crowded there as I had anticipated and I sensed people watching me. A woman asked what I was after, and as we were trying to figure out whether al-Afifi was a street or an alley, a gentleman seated on the ground, sunning himself and smoking, remarked: "She'll be one of those newspaper people, come to take her photos and fuck off."

Politely, as though I hadn't heard, I asked him if he knew where I might find the tomb of Rashid Pasha in al-Afifi. "There are no Afifis here, but there's Abou Aouf's court. I'll take you if you want."

Better I find my own way, I thought, but I made a mental note to refer to a court not a tomb the next time I asked for directions. If I didn't find Enayat today, she would send me a sign when she was ready.

I wandered aimlessly, peering through the entrances to the courts and up at the family names over their lintels. I didn't mean to spy, but every step I took delivered me countless scenes from their interiors. I was in a strange mood. Not frustrated exactly, because Enayat had taught me over the years that nothing about her would ever come easily. Nor did the traduced beauty of these tombs inspire any sense of sorrow in me or moral judgment on the living occupants who disturbed the rest of the dead. I couldn't remember which of my friends had once described his mood as "pins and needles," but it fitted perfectly.

Around me, the living were sleeping and waking, eating and bickering and breeding. It was somehow ugly to witness, painful even, a scene better not seen at all, yet at the same time, it offered powerful evidence of a will to live, of their resolve. Passing by the incised names—bedrooms, kitchens, and washing tubs all open and spilling onto the street, the electric cables strung tight across Kufic calligraphy (*And every soul shall taste death*)—my initial shock shaded into familiarity. Cactuses next to dried flowers next to mounds of rubbish, the smell of piss and fried garlic. Barefoot children scampering, one in an Adidas T-shirt. A gas range set on a grave. A washing line slung from tree trunk to marble headstone. Mayada al-Hennawy singing "I adore you" . . . and, despite the chill, beneath a tree that fronted the green of a finely worked iron gate, a knot of men all smoking in their underwear, white shorts and vests and nothing else besides, as though lounging by an invisible seashore.

As I went, my mind began to wander with me. A memory of the last time I'd been to the cemetery in Basateen. It was back in 1995, not a funeral but a wedding, whose I don't know, but the Sufi praise-singer Sheikh Yassin al-Tohamy had performed. That night it had seemed the most beautiful place in the world. A summer breeze, the distant lights from the top of Mokattam's cliff face, strangers holding out hands that held fat joints, and the rasp of al-Tohamy's voice: "What good be there in love if it should spare the heart?" I had floated motionless for hours, that extraordinary sensation of being cut off from past and present. Not of going away, exactly, not of traveling, but rather that you're flying: a flight which ends with the end of the night.

The day after my walkabout, I had a taxi drop me off on Sixteen Street. I passed the shoppers and the sellers, the pavements and the walls of the courts covered with goods and every conceivable kind of scrap and appliance: VCRs and washing machines and gas bottles, window frames and bedsteads in wood and iron, aluminium cabinets and broken chairs and car tires, empty bottles that once held quality whiskey and vodka. A market for the waste disgorged from the city's guts.

I turned off one side street into another, then another, and I began to hear my own footsteps. There was no one around me, like I'd wandered into the outskirts of the City of the Dead.

I came to a great tomb towering like a castle, barred against invaders by the huge locks hanging from its gate. Through the railings I could make out cactuses and well-tended flowers and I imagined the lucky residents stepping out from their burial-chamber bedrooms at dawn to gather in the courtyard and talk.

Squabbling children brought me out of my reverie. An Adidas T-shirt again. Surely not the same child I'd seen the day before. "Adidas among the tombs . . ." came the thought, and all of a sudden I was remembering a relative of mine, a classmate back in primary school who'd become a construction worker in Cairo. One of the most intensely pious people I've ever known: gentle with his family, prays the five prayers daily, and goes into seclusion for the last ten days of Ramadan. He has never harmed a soul and to me is the model of what a true Muslim should be. I once saw him, dapper and handsome, wearing a T-shirt which bore, in English, the slogan of an abortion rights campaign from overseas: *The right to choose—It's my body!* God knows where he'd found it. I'd been unsure. Should I tell him? Did he have the right to know? A moral quandary which I settled inside a minute: I didn't say a word. And now I felt guilty.

My journey ended at a makeshift cafeteria outside the entrance to a tomb, seated on one of the red plastic chairs that were clustered beneath an ancient tree. I felt at peace, as though this little stand of chairs had always been my destination, and ordered a tea, then changed my mind, and asked for a bottle of water.

"We don't have bottled water, miss. Will you take a Pepsi?"

"Please."

A man seated beside me smiled my way, and once we had exchanged greetings, I asked him if he knew the area.

"Well I've lived here for forty years."

We chatted for a while and, emboldened, I lit myself a cigarette and another for him.

He wanted to know why I'd come and I told him that I was looking for a street called al-Afifi. An alley, perhaps.

"There's no al-Afifi here," he said. "It must be in Basateen or the Mamluk cemetery."

"This isn't Basateen?"

I must have come farther than I'd thought.

I once read that this stretch of desert was where the Mamluks held their military parades, their rites and races, feats of arms and religious feasts. They chose to be buried here because it is so dry. Amid its miles of walls and doors, the ramrod avenues and evergreen trees, outsiders quickly lose their way. Historical periods tangle, interleaving their walis and pashas, mosques and palaces, the shrines of their saints. There are no signs to mark boundaries in the City of the Dead.

I intended to resume my search the next day, convinced I must be very close to finding Enayat's grave. But this was naïve. I would finally locate Rashid Pasha's tomb in the summer of 2018, only to learn that this tomb was not the end of the trail. Enayat's resolve, it seemed, was as strong as Paula had claimed, as though she were watching over every moment of my journey and wanted me to reach her by some other road.

2.

I was woken by my phone ringing beside the bed. Half awake, with the sense of dread that presages any morning call, I reached out my hand and answered.

It was Paula, her voice unmistakable: "I know I've already put you through enough trouble, but how much longer are you going to be in Egypt? I was going to ask you to come by tomorrow evening around nine, but it won't work now. Could we meet up when you're back in the summer? The bronchitis laid me out and I'm still recovering. Faten's death affected me very badly, you see . . ."

I was fully awake.

"No, no, you must get better, ustaza . . ."

On the verge of asking her, "Who's Faten?" I realized she must be talking about the actress Faten Hamama, whose death had been widely reported the month before. And I don't know what I said for the remainder of our conversation, only that no sooner was it over than I flung open the door to the balcony, stared out at Cairo, and cried, "Finally!"

The aunts, back at my grandfather's house for their summer break: urbanized students in short nightgowns, watching the late-night film on the black-and-white set in the television room, hair curlers doubling the size of their heads.

The television is showing *Sleepless*. My aunts sip lemon juice from tall ribbed glasses; on-screen, Faten Hamama and Emad Hamdy play Nadia and Mustafa. They are speaking on the phone:

"Well, my name is Nadia Lutfi, and my father is Ahmed Lutfi. I live in Dokki. You know who I am and I know you fancy me. Oh, and you kicked a football at me this morning. That enough for you?"

Nadia arranges to meet Mustafa outside the Equestrian Club at four thirty the following afternoon.

Then an exterior scene: Nadia Lutfi, walking along the outer wall of the club. She wears white gloves and a sleeveless dress that might be pink, or maybe rose, and is covered in little white circles.

"Such a pretty dress," says the youngest aunt.

"We've got eyes too, you know," the eldest replies.

As they bicker, Nadia's lines, delivered in formal Arabic, are moving me to tears:

"I am bewildered. Lost. I feel a mysterious hand propelling me towards a fate that is no more certain. And I feel that I need somebody by my side, a person to direct me and guide me down the path of safety. But there is no one.

"I cannot ask my father or his wife for advice.

"I feel the same loneliness as before, and I am afraid of Mustafa. He is stronger than I am, and older. More experienced. Should I go home? I should go home!"

But before she can make her mind up, Mustafa's convertible pulls up beside her, and the relationship begins.

Standing there on the balcony, looking out at the city, I thought of that world: the dome of Cairo University, the private clubs and peaceful neighborhood parks, open-topped cars and black-and-white TVs, short skirts and cocktail parties. I thought of how my aunts, too, must have longed to be stars of the screen. For sure that desire was there, at least before kids and work and the hijab put paid to it.

Cinema held out the promise of an alternative geography. Its dramatic denouements offered hope for a different life. Cairo of the fifties and sixties. Rebellious girls filling journals with roses printed on their covers and falling for the wrong men—for older men, for men who are poorer than them, or richer. Girls harboring secrets which others expose as the crisis draws near. And then the men, wedded to distance, who are posted to Egypt's deep south or sent to study in Europe, whose credulity when faced with slander is the torment of their lovers, who are sometimes killed in battle.

These films were a window on love, misfortune, and retribution. There was always retribution, if not from society, then from the skies.

The night before Paula's morning call, I did as I'd done every day since my arrival in Cairo, and tried to call her. And, as usual, she hadn't answered. The frustrations I had managed to hold at bay over the last few days then swept over me:

I had foregone a planned visit to Egypt a year and a half before, then taken up the opportunities afforded by a semester-long sabbatical and an invitation to Italy, just so I could meet Paula now. Here I was, hostage to fortune, my evenings left open on the off chance she might call, only going out when all hope was lost. This whole trip had been a waste of time, I told myself. Nothing had come of it. I needed connections to get into the state archives and track down Rashid Pasha. No one in the City of the Dead knew where the al-Afifi cemetery was. In Dokki, it transpired, there was no such place as Astra Square!

And Paula wasn't answering.

More burdensome than the frustration was having to confront the questions I'd been putting off: What was it I was looking for, exactly? I mean, I had no idea what I was going to do with the photographs and papers that Paula had promised me—supposing I ever got them. Was I running away, escaping my own life by chasing clues into the life of a woman who wrote a single novel and died before she could see it published? Hadn't I read her novel several times already? How significant a novel was it, anyway? Enough for me to go searching for its author? Was it her decision to end her life that drew me to her, or the thought of her unrealized potential?

Hadn't Paula already told me enough over the course of our phone calls for me to picture her life?

The night before, as I'd first kindled then luxuriated in my anger, it had never occurred to me that Faten Hamama's death might have something to do with Paula's inexplicable disappearance. But this morning, the connection seemed to offer access to the very world I longed for like a child. After all, who didn't know that Paula had taken her screen name Nadia Lutfi from the role Faten played in *Sleepless*? Hadn't Paula told me that she and Enayat had hopeless crushes on Faten, and that Paula and her husband had watched the film with Enayat at Cinema Miami in December 1957?

Back in from the balcony, I made coffee, then opened my file on Paula to transcribe what I could remember of our conversation before it slipped away. She had told me a tale. A tale she'd told many times before in interviews, with slight variations every time.

Her decision to work in cinema, she said, caused strain at home, and her parents made her promise that if she was going to be an actress, she wouldn't use the family name. There were other considerations, too: Paula might sound strange to ears attuned to more common Egyptian names. The producer Ramses Naguib had suggested Samiha Hussein as a screen name, but she didn't like it. After one particularly difficult night it struck her that the confusion she felt was much like that of Nadia, the heroine in *Sleepless*, when she says: "I've been through hard times, and my hope's begun to drift and fade, till all I can see of it is a mirage, a distant shadow."

Paula made up her mind that the crisis facing the character Nadia Lutfi suited her perfectly.

And she called Enayat:

"Hello? How are you, Ninou? Do you have *Sleepless* by Ihsan Abdel Quddous?"

"Does it have to be Ihsan? I've got other books. Good ones."

"No, it has to be that one."

"I don't have it."

"Fine, but if you happen to come across it, buy it and bring it round."

"Paula, what's going on?"

"Nothing, the same old trouble at home."

"The family still not supporting our young starlet's dreams?"

"Very funny. We'll talk when you come round."

"Don't worry, Paula."

"I'll wait for you. Don't be late."

Paula had the most extraordinary ability to summon Enayat al-Zayyat's voice out of decades of silence.

When I returned that summer, I told myself, I would visit Paula's apartment for the first time. Enayat's friend! It wouldn't be just Paula I would meet there, in other words, but also the actress Nadia Lutfi and her creations: Ahlam from *The Seven Daughters*, Mady from *Sunglasses*, Soheir from *The Sins*, the Ilham and Mustafa double act from *For Men Only*, Riri in *Autumn Quail*, Louisa in *Saladin*, Zouba the dancer in *Palace of Desire*, Zaina the matriarch in *The Mummy*, Ferdous in *My Father Up the Tree,* as well as all the women whose lives she'd worn in her middle age, characters whose names and films had slipped my mind, but who all wore wigs and plucked their eyebrows into oblivion. I would meet them all.

It was my last day in Cairo. I decided that I wouldn't be going to the tombs.

3.

Love and Silence . . .

I came across *Love and Silence* in 1993, during a hunt for a cheap copy of *Collected Miracles*, al-Nabhani's dictionary of holy men. "One pound," said the bookseller by the Ezbekiya wall, and though I'd never heard of it before, I bought it on the spot.

From her name I instantly assumed that the author must be the younger sister of the activist and writer Latifa al-Zayyat.

The United Arab Republic—Ministry of Culture
Love and Silence—An Egyptian Novel
Enayat al-Zayyat
Dar al-Katib al-Arabi (AH 1386 / AD 1967)
Introduction by Mustafa Mahmoud

The novel opens in Cairo, as the narrator describes her state of mind following her brother's death in November 1950:

And again I was overcome by the piercing realization that, with his death and departure, this incredibly precious thing had vanished from my life: that I had lost my brother.

Hisham has died in an accident on the parallel bars, a discipline of which he says, *It gives me control over my body.* Hisham's absence is a fount, the spring from which the narrative flows, branching into a tangle of internal reflections, among them the narrator's account of her depression and her meditations on the meaning of a life lived in the presence of death:

And I looked into his face, unable to believe that Hisham could be dead, that this face would forever be a sleeper's. A sleeper without breath in his chest. Yet at the same time, the lack of breath seemed meaningless, like he could get to his feet, and run about, and laugh; that he was stronger than anyone, than everyone, and didn't need something as insubstantial as breath to live. And I reached out my hands and ran them over his face, maybe so he might feel them and open his eyes to me—me, his sister, Najla. But the face stayed still and frozen. I thought I saw a blue steal into his lips, then seep slowly outwards across his features, and for the first time I found myself afraid of him, and ashamed of myself for my fear; for fearing my brother now that his soul was gone. I felt as though I was spying on someone I didn't know. Then I saw him, or imagined I saw him, turn his face from me, and the sight was insupportable, because for the first time I had accepted his death.

The reader learns of the narrator's grief and her brother's death before they know what to call her. During the course of an earlier scene in which her perspective is intercut with those of the other characters around her, and up until this unbroken train of thought as she stands over her brother's corpse, she never tells us her name. Hisham's death is presented as a first step to understanding:

In my mind, brooding on death and dwelling on my brother's name grew interchangeable. I thought of him as a territory, its shores uncharted, ringed by mystery. Whoever discovers these shores never returns.

I expected the book to develop into an elegy for the dead brother, or to take us through the narrator's gradual emergence from grief. And so it did, briefly, but at the same time, and imperceptibly, it was generating layers, complex and overlapping: every bid to escape her state of mourning becomes entangled with a fresh challenge and prompts a return to the cocoon of that inner voice.

For instance, against the wishes of her family, Najla takes a job, but quickly finds herself unhappy and questioning the worth of what she does. She wonders about her family and her place amid its cold bourgeois detachment when she realizes that her bedroom contains more tokens of love affairs and friendships than anything which links her to her parents.

Then there is the evolution of her political awareness, a process which begins when she meets a writer and revolutionary called Ahmed. She starts to adopt his views on colonialism, poverty, and the corruption of the royal family, and then looks deeper, into the selfishness of her own social class and the responsibility it bears for the ills of the status quo. Here, Najla makes her most forceful break with the gravities of Hisham's death, when she realizes that her brother—a pampered, bourgeois university student—had been deeply self-centered and trivial:

Had I really loved him, or was I merely expected to, like everyone else in the family? How did such a simple, obvious truth pass me by?

Only now do I see that I had never been more than Hisham's lackey; what happiness I knew was only spillover from his greater store, and all the joys of home life were because of him and for his sake.

We are repeatedly taken beyond the tragedy of Hisham's death, beyond remembrance and wrestling with loss, into a taxonomy of the different routes to freedom—employment, love, political consciousness—but each attempt carries within it the inevitability of her return to a cycle of depression and isolation. It is as though there is something wrong with Najla, a flaw she carries with her as she shuttles back and forth, in and out of life, and which poisons everything she tries.

The novel ends in a great confusion. In fact, it's as though there are four distinct endings set alongside one another in the space of a few pages:

One: Ahmed, the revolutionary lover who encouraged her fledgling political consciousness, falls ill and goes abroad to begin treatment. Najla learns to make peace with the world and to live with herself, and, through the support she gives to Ahmed in his illness, she learns to give.

Two: Ahmed returns from his treatment abroad and their relationship peters out. Najla starts to enjoy her own company. She takes walks through the places where they used to meet and realizes that a man should be a part of a woman's life, not life itself. She applies to the College of Fine Arts—and buys a set of new curtains.

Three: Ahmed travels abroad for a second round of treatment, and dies. We are now faced with the possibility of a second wave of mourning, but Najla goes to university all the same: she wants to paint, for her life to have meaning.

Four: The final ending takes up less than a single page: a brief description of the 1952 revolution, presented as the happy ending our narrator deserves after her long and painful journey.

All these endings work as conclusions to Najla's journey, but the first three are plausible extensions of her quest for identity, and for all that they involve Ahmed's illness (and the end of her relationship with him and his death), they also offer closure, because Najla is permitted to create new possibilities for her future. The fourth is genuinely problematic, not just because the solution it provides comes from outside the narrative, and not because it is indistinguishable from the clichéd conclusions of many novels written in the aftermath of 1952, but because of its language. The language is a puzzle. It feels as though the author has begun her journey with the whisper of an inner voice, like someone peering through the window of her bedroom at the bleak emptiness of the streets outside, and that she has retained this voice throughout, for all that it is shaped and changed by experience and engagement with other people, only for it to suddenly vanish, its place taken by something sonorous and depersonalized.

For the last ten lines it is the masses that speak, and the book's very last sentence is its worst:

The clank of the tank tracks shook the ground, and as I stood there, smiling, the new day began to dawn.

The lack of clarity is a curiosity too. Are these multiple endings intended as a satirical comment on the very idea of a conclusion, or had their young and inexperienced author, caught between these options, decided that she would leave it to her readers to resolve an ending for her?

It wasn't what happened in the novel that made me fall in love with it. Even in 1993, callow as I was, I knew that a good novel is more than the sum of its incidents. Nor was I drawn to it because of its social or feminist "consciousness," or the simple historical fact that it had been written by a young woman in the 1960s. As a matter of fact, at that time in my life, in conversation with friends and fellow writers I would frequently mock the idea of describing a novel as "conscious" or praising a work of literature simply because it "reflected reality" or championed a particular social class, or issue, or nation. And we reserved our profoundest mockery for any defense of "higher values" in incompetent literature.

Back then, I was the same as all my friends. We read "high literature" (defined by consensus), but we also read randomly, hunting out whatever appealed to us around the margins of this definition. My passions included C. P. Cavafy, Wadie Saadeh, Yehia Haqqi, Régis Debray, Samir Amin, Tzvetan Todorov, Eduardo Galeano, Milan Kundera, Louis Awad, and more, and I would argue for my choices with a partisan's fervor:

"How can you even mention al-Aqqad alongside Taha Hussein?"

"Critics need to read Abdelfattah Kilito."

"Sepúlveda's *The Old Man Who Read Love Stories* is better than *One Hundred Years of Solitude.*"

"So the Ministry of Culture can invite Darwish and Adonis, but not Sargon Boulus?"

A young woman writer had to personally celebrate the books which "touched" her, as though she needed to define herself by appending her discoveries to the canon.

I added *Love and Silence* to the great chain.

The language in *Love and Silence* is both fresh and refreshing. Sometimes cold, sometimes sentimental, it can feel uncanny, too, as though translated. Occasionally you sense the ponderous influence of contemporary romance novels, but elsewhere it is modern, strange, limpid, and beyond categorization. It is clearly a first work, but its tonal inconsistencies are held together by virtue of the author's talent. In a single paragraph, the reader might encounter a wide sample of registers, the spectrum of the author's language choices:

Out of the still calm of sleep I pulled myself into motion, wandered across the room and, standing by the window, brushed my discontent into the street. I sat down—looked out—paged through the book of life. My heart was heavy and to my eyes everything seemed old. People were damp yellow leaves and I was unmoved by them, by their faces, by the soft covers of their clothes. I felt at once imprisoned by this life and pulled towards new horizons. I wanted to pull this self clear, gummy with the sap of its surroundings; to tear free into a wider world. The clear skies of my country bored me. I wanted others, dark and muddied and threatening, capable of stirring fear and astonishment. I wanted my feet to know a different land.

As soon as I finished a first reading of *Love and Silence*, I turned back and began again. In my notebook, I copied out passages, small stand-alone texts like lights to illuminate my emotional state:

I am in exile from myself. Who can issue a pardon for my soul, so that it might return, might know the body as its own small true homeland? [. . .] If I were able, I would erase myself and be reborn, somewhere else, some other time. Another time. Another time . . . Was I born at the wrong time, maybe?

Sometimes a piece of writing can shake your very being. This doesn't mean it has to be unprecedented in the history of literature or the best thing you've ever read. It is fate, delivering a message to help you make sense of whatever you're going through—and at the exact moment you most need it, whether you realize it or not. We are grateful, not only to "great" literature, but to all writing which plays a significant role in how we understand ourselves in a particular moment. When we turn to contemplate our lives, it is these works that let us see.

Love and Silence is a novel about death. Not Hisham's death, nor the death of her lover, Ahmed, but the quotidian death against which Najla goes to war within herself. Her life becomes unbearable, her every escape attempt falling back into routine and ennui, from taking the job she had hoped would be her gateway to the world, to the love and freedom that leaves her unmoored and at a loss. Najla is depressed, insomniac, alienated. She feels not only born out of time, but that she isn't functioning as she should. There is a bedspread missing a final stitch, a canvas unfinished on the easel: she never finishes what she's started. Ahmed helps Najla confront her paralysis. With teasing affection he dedicates his book to:

The reader who doesn't read, the painter who doesn't paint.

Najla has no idea how to live without keeping herself under observation. What is captivating about the novel is the author's desire to document this internal journey and the language in which she does it. It is a personal journey, a quest for meaning, and the novel's themes—employment, love, the politics of class and country and colonialism, and her naïve rejoicing over the 1952 revolution that we encounter in its final paragraph—are all thresholds which lie outside herself and which she must cross. The voice shows us more when it speaks out of the interior darkness.

My conviction that Enayat was Latifa al-Zayyat's younger sister remained unchallenged. It even grew stronger: I began to imagine that I could see the influence of the elder sister on her sibling.

Latifa was born in 1923 and Enayat, though I didn't know her date of birth, must have been around ten years younger. While Latifa was making her name as a leader of the Higher Committee of Students and Workers in 1946—the senior members of her family fretting over her behavior and her future—the teenage Enayat was torn between her love of Cairo's members' clubs, its singers and cinema, and her desire to become a daring political leader like her sister.

In 1952, Latifa married the playwright Rashad Rushdi. For more than a decade thereafter she stepped away from the struggle. But Enayat grew bolder and declared that she was a poet. Her poems weren't much, just thoughts jotted down without any attention paid to technique and craft, but though Latifa wasn't keen on them, Rushdi supported her. He even made the girl a present of his copy of Nizar Qabbani's collection *You Are Mine*. When Latifa's *The Open*

Door was published in 1960, followed three years later by the film, Enayat decided that she had something new to say about discontent and depression and death, and the only way she could ever say these things in a debut novel would be by doing what was expected of any self-respecting author: she must link her personal story to public concerns. It would be decades before any talented woman author in Egypt was able to tell her story without reflexively asserting an equivalence with wider societal issues, because *The Open Door* was so dominant a model.

A convincing story. But in her memoirs, *The Search: Personal Papers* (1992), though Latifa talks a lot about her two brothers and the men in her life, she only mentions, very fleetingly, a single sister called Safiya. So Enayat had to be reassigned: a younger cousin.

In December 1997, I submitted my MA thesis on Adonis, and the novelist Radwa Ashour asked me to provide her with the Sufi sources I'd used in my research. I brought a box of books over to Radwa's house and drank tea with her and her husband, the poet Mourid al-Barghouti, and as we sat, I unpacked the books. Nearly all were old and yellowed, with the green cover of al-Nabhani's *Collected Miracles* shining brightly among them. I asked her if she'd heard of a novelist by the name of Enayat al-Zayyat, and was she a relative of Latifa's? And Radwa said that, unless I knew better, she didn't believe they were related at all. She added that she had heard Enayat's father was from the al-Zayyat family in Mansoura and that her mother had possibly been German.

4.

The introduction to *Love and Silence* had been written by Dr. Mustafa Mahmoud. Truth be told it wasn't any kind of introduction at all, either to the novel or its author, but rather a mere four and a half pages which begin:

I was leafing through a strange book, reading its dreamlike sentences and trying to picture the woman who had written it. It dripped with delicacy and sweetness.

Then, after having offered a selection of what he judges to be the novel's most delicate turns of phrase, he concludes his introduction with four lines of his own:

This elegant book, Love and Silence, *is the first and last that its gifted author, Enayat al-Zayyat, ever wrote, for she died a young woman, still in her twenties. The agonies of her brilliant heart and her own tortured humanity were too much for her to bear. May God multiply blessings on her pure spirit and her elevated art.*

Better we don't spend too long on Mustafa Mahmoud's depiction of the author. To this day, Arab authors continue to betray their personal convictions through the language they use. The only way for a woman to write well is delicately and sweetly.

But the introduction raises other questions: How did she die? When? Why does *Love and Silence* remain outside the canons of contemporary literature and women's writing in Arabic? Is it perhaps because, with it coming out just seven years after *The Open Door*, readers could not appreciate its unique qualities? Or was it that it was published in 1967, the year of Egypt's defeat by Israel, and no one read it at all? Unlike Latifa, Enayat was never affiliated with the Egyptian Left. Did the Left use its cultural influence to exclude her from consideration?

And then, why was Mustafa Mahmoud chosen to write the introduction? Had Enayat asked him to do it before she died? Did the publisher genuinely believe he was the literary celebrity best placed to understand and present her work?

Although Mustafa Mahmoud (1921–2009) was indeed a literary figure of some repute in the 1960s, he has never been near any list of great Arabic literature. Prior to this I hadn't read a word he'd written. My knowledge of him began and ended with *Science and Faith*, a television program he hosted, and the mosque which bears his name in Arab League Street. But for Enayat's sake, I read what I could of his pre-1967 work.

His short stories, like "Eating Bread" and "The Smell of Blood," seemed to me more like synopses of full-length novels, and were heavily didactic too, as though he'd never encountered the prose of writers like Yehia Haqqi, Yusuf Idris, or Naguib Mahfouz. I read the popular essays which were probably the source of his fame, all about God and Man and the Devil and the Riddle of Death. I even went so far as to read his novel, *The Impossible* (1960), in search of any intersection between his fictional universe and Enayat's.

The protagonist of *The Impossible*, Hilmi, has an overbearing father, but when the father dies, our hero starts gambling on the stock exchange and going out to nightclubs. He is seduced by Fatima, a lawyer and friend of his wife, but soon tires of their relationship and starts another affair with his neighbor's wife, Nani. He cannot decide whether to sell off his father's land in the south, or use it to grow onions. Hilmi may be a paper-thin creation—as are all the characters in *The Impossible*—but the narrative weaves in shreds of philosophical and existential readings which lend it the illusion of depth.

Mustafa Mahmoud was about as far as one could get from *Love and Silence* and its language.

There's a kind of intense curiosity which possesses us when we encounter an author who is truly unknown—a branch cut from the tree with no date of birth or death in evidence—or when their writing offers no clues to the wider life of their generation, to their close friends or literary influences.

Writers are solitary creatures, sure, but they work with a language that others also use, and it is impossible to conceive of any writing that takes place in complete isolation. So who did Enayat read? Mustafa Mahmoud? And, of her contemporaries, who read her drafts, or sat with her to discuss ideas about craft? Did she know any writers who were active at the time, or was she on the margins of the historical moment which shaped them all?

Before Enayat's ghost began to pursue me in earnest, before I gave myself over entirely to retracing her steps, I was still no more than a reader, someone looking to fit this unknown woman into my literary family tree. When I first started thinking about *Love and Silence* I had turned to my readings of Foucault and his theory of the archive. I assumed that understanding Enayat's book would mean analyzing the text's discursive formation—the historical a prioris that, collectively, make the existence of its words possible—along with the types of dissolution that lay behind its unusual publishing trajectory, its reception, and its subsequent marginalization in Arabic literary culture. It was the society of texts generated by women Arab writers prior to the publication of *Love and Silence* in 1967 that would intersect with and shed light on this novel as a historical moment. In other words, I had to read dozens of stories and novels from the mid-nineteenth century onwards. The literary value of some of these books has expired with the social or political function for which they were produced. With others, their significance is preserved in academic surveys and inventories which document the literary output of women from the start of the Nahda, the so-called Arab Renaissance of the late nineteenth century, even though the only people who still read them are academics. Then there are those which cling shyly on at the margins of the literary mainstream; of these, a very few continue to be read and to exert power and influence.

I took it as axiomatic that Latifa al-Zayyat's *The Open Door* represents what Edward Said terms *the determining imprint*, the influence individual books can have on *an otherwise anonymous collective body of texts* whose unity is created by the fact of their interreference. But Enayat's voice, the whisper that never speaks to the masses, the hesitant, melancholy, unconfident murmur, like weeping heard on the other side of a wall, this voice which seems to have come adrift from poetry and which poetry alone might have been able to rescue—this voice seems out of place in the community of texts to which *The Open Door* belongs. More than that, impossibly, it seems to be entirely obscure, as if it had no influence on what was written afterwards, as if it had never been heard.

On March 18, 1967, the eminent critic Anis Mansour wrote an article in the Cairo-based newspaper, *al-Akhbar*. The title of the article is "Yet Her Book Was Published Years After Her Death" and it opens as follows:

She showed us her modest literary output—a collection of articles, a collection of short stories, and some essays on books she was reading—and waited for me to give my opinion on what she had written and what she had read. She used to go to her father and get him to buy her books by the hundred and shut herself away to think in silence. Then, from nowhere, she decided to write a novel, her only novel, which was published just yesterday with the title Love and Silence. *I never dreamed that when I gave her my support she would rush to death, taking with her all the gifts and fineness of feeling she possessed. She gave me an early draft of this first novel written in lead pencil, and I told her to go ahead and finish it without regard to proper grammar and spelling: These are little things, easily corrected! Write! Write! She completed the book in late 1961 and sent it to al-Qawmiyya, the publishers. And at al-Qawmiyya the novel encountered desk after desk, then desk drawer after desk drawer, before preceding its author to the dusty grave of the archive's shelves.*

Then it was plucked from this dust, tasted gingerly by lemon-sour lips, and a decision taken that it was not fit to publish. Empty, cruel heads nodded sagely, and finally, eventually, agreed that it should be returned. And so the novel came home.

Mansour devotes the greater part of his article to an overview of the novel's plot and excerpts, but here and there, amongst it all, he presents us with what seem to be facts about Enayat:

- That he sent her his notes on the draft novel and that she rejected them. He promised to send her novel and other writings on to his contacts, but never met her again.
- That he heard from her friend, the actress Nadia Lutfi, that Enayat had completed the novel and was working at the German Institute, and was very happy there. Although he couldn't remember just when this conversation with Nadia Lutfi had taken place, he states with some conviction that she had completed the novel in late 1961.
- That Enayat struggled in Arabic: her schooling had been in German.
- That as part of a delegation of writers which went to Yemen in 1963, he had to share a room with Youssef al-Sebaie. The room was extremely hot, and Mansour quoted a line from Enayat's novel as the perfect description of the stifling atmosphere—*everything halted, all meaning froze, each minute transformed into an eternal jail cell*—only to discover that al-Sebaie knew her too, and had read her writing and promised to get her published. It was al-Sebaie who told him she was dead.

- That Enayat's father, Abbas al-Zayyat, had told him that she'd refused to self-publish the novel. Al-Qawmiyya's rejection had come as a violent shock. It had silenced her completely and she had stopped speaking or reading or writing. Her family had felt that she was settling her account with the world.
- That she had taken twenty sleeping pills and that when her family found her on January 5, 1963, she had been dead for twenty-four hours.
- That she had left three sheets of paper beside the bed. One bore the words, *My darling son, Abbas, farewell. I do love you, it's just that life is unbearable. Forgive me.*

The article was treasure. I read it over and over, as though at any moment I might uncover yet another secret buried between its lines. The idea that a young woman would kill herself—a young woman with a son, a father, and a best friend—and all because of a book, was genuinely tragic, but it was also seductive in its tragedy. I pictured Enayat painstakingly acquiring the rudiments of good Arabic grammar and inflection, then carefully setting down everything she wanted to say in her novel, then refusing the suggestion that she should self-publish.

Enayat resembled her narrator, Najla, but Najla's pursuit of an identity through work and love and politics had ended in hope, in the July Revolution and the tanks rolling through the streets as *the new day began to dawn*. Enayat's journey through writing had ended in despair, rejected by a publishing house that was itself a creation of the revolution. I saw Enayat as the protagonist of her own private psychodrama, in which writing was her identity and the only way she might find meaning. The rejection of the novel had meant identity thrown into doubt and meaning lost.

I wondered: Did Anis Mansour feel guilty at all? Then I reminded myself that she never gave him her novel once she'd completed it, that she hadn't asked him to help her publish it, nor sought his help after al-Qawmiyya had rejected her.

This was her decision, then: not to turn to him again.

But following her death Mansour would offer up Enayat to his readership repeatedly, recirculating these same facts in article after article, sometimes adding details, sometimes amending what he'd said before.

For instance, in 2006 he wrote a piece in the *al-Sharq al-Awsat* newspaper—"*Love and Silence*: O Grief!"—in which he tells us that he first met Enayat in the company of up-and-coming star Nadia Lutfi in the home of Mrs. Wigdan al-Barbary, owner of the largest equestrian stables in Egypt. Nadia and Enayat had been whispering to one another in German, and when they realized that Mansour spoke it too, the conversation became general. He states that Enayat gave him some short stories, and that he published them; that he didn't like their sense of futility, of the hopelessness of life. He repeats the claim that he suggested some changes to the novel, but that she had turned them down:

I proposed one change, that she make the opening of the novel its conclusion, then suggested that she give her protagonists the chance to speak for themselves, and not press her own words onto their tongues and into their ears, and so stand in the way of their journey. It was as though she was reluctant to grant her characters the freedom which eluded her. I told her, If I'd written this story, I would have said this, and removed that, and added this, but don't do what I tell you. After all, I'm not you, and you aren't me. Your dress wouldn't work as my suit, and my suit wouldn't suit as a swimming costume.

Then he states that she had handed him some rough drafts of her short stories, and that when he revisited them after her death he decided there would be no point in publishing them after all.

In 2010, he added two new details to the story in Stations, his weekly column in *al-Ahram*. The first was that he had published some of her stories in *al-Jeel* magazine in 1960, while the second explained why Mustafa Mahmoud wrote the introduction to her novel:

I heard that she had passed the novel to Dr. Mustafa Mahmoud. He took his own view: it seems that he regarded it, not in terms of craft or philosophy, but like a surgeon. Had he been too harsh when he gave her his advice? Surely she was in no need of more anxiety and sleepless nights while she waited for him to write to her with his assessment of the novel, while she waited for him to write his introduction?

Enayat seems to haunt Mansour, who continues to summon her memory in a range of different contexts. For instance, he references her in his discussion of young women writers who emerged in the 1950s, whom he saw as moving women's literature away from "delicacy" and starting to show their "claws":

The windows were flung open to a bracing new breeze, to fresh scents, to cries of the crowd and revolution, to a literature with claws

that tore Love and Evil and Life into ribbons and scratched the face
of Man the Provider, man who denies woman her freedom.

He remembers her again in the course of his account of
the murder of Afghan poet Nadia Anjuman by her husband:

My friendship with Enayat al-Zayyat was long and profound.
I read everything she wrote, and myself published her only novel, her
last sad cry. I still have her handwritten manuscript . . .

In which way, through Mansour's retelling, Enayat
becomes an archetype, the figure he gestures to whenever
he wants to discuss women's writing, or suicide, or murder,
or any of the strange and marvelous things he may have
witnessed in the course of his life. A prolific columnist
writing with such glib facility about a dead woman none
of his readers have heard of. So fascinated is he by her story
that he always has something to say about it, even though
his actual view remains unchanged. However, in death their
relationship evolves: from that of a young woman writer
soliciting a literary star for his opinions, to one of profound
friendship.

From what he writes, we learn that Mansour read *Love*
and Silence in 1960, then suggested changes to the manuscript
which the author turned down. He made no attempt to publish the book after her suicide even though the manuscript,
handwritten in lead pencil, was in his possession. And though
he tells us that he knew her father, the provost of Cairo
University, he never seems to have asked him if there was
a second, edited manuscript in existence. He had her short
stories, but thought there would be no point in publishing
them, because the writer had silenced herself.

And we learn that Youssef al-Sebaie had also read the novel and had promised to help her get it published.

As for Mustafa Mahmoud: according to Mansour he read the novel and then Enayat waited for him to write an introduction, but he never did.

So Mansour's use of the first-person plural—*She showed us her modest literary output*—could be seen as referring not only to himself, but to al-Sebaie and Mahmoud as well. Why, I asked myself, had Enayat shown her novel to three of the most widely read and distributed authors of the day, and those furthest removed from her own literary sensibilities? If it was a question of fame, then why not take it to Ihsan Abdel Quddous, who outsold everyone? Was it admiration for what they wrote that prompted her to turn to them? Perhaps a belief that they promoted young authors? Or was her connection to Arabic-language literary culture so tenuous that she simply didn't know anyone else?

Anis Mansour and Mustafa Mahmoud worked in journalism and shared an interest in philosophy. Their books were published by Dar al-Maaref. Mustafa Mahmoud didn't like the novel, and showed no interest in it or its author during her life, but after her suicide he wrote the introduction. Maybe he had softened; maybe in death the surgeon's scalpel cut less deep.

The novels of Youssef al-Sebaie—a military man of letters, who had been appointed secretary-general of the Supreme Council for Oversight of the Arts, Literatures, and Social

Sciences in 1956—would first be serialized in newspapers and magazines, then in the blink of an eye they would appear in volumes published by al-Khanji or Dar al-Fikr al-Arabi before making their way seamlessly onto the silver screen.

What stroke of fortune brought Enayat into contact with these literary stars? I tried to picture myself in her situation, exactly thirty years on, "showing my literary output" to three men like these three and waiting for their "support."

Except, by 1990, there were no stars of their caliber, and no readership like that which they'd enjoyed.

I looked in *al-Jeel*. There were no stories by Enayat al-Zayyat, not in 1960, and not before or afterwards, either. I noticed that every time Mansour mentioned Enayat, he followed it with a sentence that hinted as much. Take this, from 2006:

Enayat placed a full stop at the end of the sentence: a zero at the end of a life that meant so much more than zero, but she was gone without ever finding this out!

Or this, from 2010, where he ended an article declaring her *an artist who had no sooner appeared than she disappeared herself, forever! She died without trace!*

Of course I felt angry. Not so much because Mansour placed the responsibility for Enayat's disappearance on herself and framed her tracelessness as its natural consequence, but because of the ease with which he repeatedly asserted it. In any case, I was happy that Enayat hadn't gone back to him after he had promised to "introduce her and her work" to his readers.

5.

Najla's closest friend in *Love and Silence* is called Nadia. They have been friends since school. Nadia supports Najla through her depression, is always coming round to see her at home, encourages her to get a job. At times, it feels as though Nadia is Najla's sole connection with the outside world. Witness Najla's constant fretting about her friend's availability:

Nadia didn't have time to waste with me anymore. Her work was constantly present, even in those moments when she should be relaxing. And if she did come round to talk, again it would only ever be about the work . . .

Evidence, as far as I was concerned, of the truth of what Anis Mansour had written: that Enayat and Nadia Lutfi were friends. I thought of them both. First Nadia, busy filming *My Only Love* in 1960, or *Don't Put Out the Sun* in 1961, or *The Sins* in 1962. And then Enayat: staying at her father's house in Dokki with her son, taking herself to the German Archaeological Institute by day, and in the evenings, as she waits for Nadia to call, editing her novel. A phrase here, a sentence there. I imagine her spending nights in sleepless anticipation of the introduction from Mustafa Mahmoud, due any day now, and waiting to hear from al-Qawmiyya.

And every now and again, of course, Nadia would come to see her, and always with stories, funny and fascinating: how she'd stood there face-to-face with Omar al-Sharif in *My Only Love*; how she'd abandoned Ramses Naguib, the producer who'd given her a debut in *Sultan*, for Dollar Film run by Gamal al-Leithy; how she had to fly up to Alexandria where her son Ahmed lived with his grandmother.

I began to see that the Enayat of my imagination was no more than a wraith, visible only in the light given off by Nadia. Nadia was someone I knew without realizing that I knew her. There were so many articles about her, so many interviews with her. And Nadia was more than simply busy: ever since entering the world of cinema, she had been in a state of transformation and flux. Her current project was a film based on Ihsan Abdel Quddous's novel *The Dark Glasses*, for which she was taking dance lessons and making weekly visits to Wigdan al-Barbary's stables in the district of Mansouriya, where she was learning to ride. This equestrian training was being overseen by the director Youssef Chahine himself, who was preparing for his epic *Saladin*.

That Nadia was Nadia was no coincidence. Enayat, like Najla, was facing down the black dog of depression, and Nadia Lutfi did indeed stay by her side despite a full and consuming life as a rising star. The novel even contains an exchange between Najla and Nadia which I can easily imagine as having taken place in reality some time in 1960:

"Nadia, you know I envy you, right?"

Nadia chuckled.

"But that's wonderful. It means you're on your way to being cured. If you can envy now, then tomorrow you'll be able to love."

First of all, I contacted the administrator of a Facebook page titled "Internationally Acclaimed Arab Equestrian Wigdan al-Barbary." He wrote back: *I've spoken with Wigdan and she tells me she doesn't remember anything. She doesn't remember anything about it.*

I spent hours browsing through photos of Wigdan with her horses, from the age of seventeen through all the international prizes she had won, then read the interviews where she spoke about the unique bond she shared with her animals.

I wrote to her secretary and told her my story, and she told me that Madame Wigdan remembered Nadia Lutfi training with her and visiting the stables in the company of Youssef Chahine, Anis Mansour, and Ahmed Ragab. She had only met Enayat twice, but she had a photograph of her and she would try and find it. She recommended asking Nadia Lutfi.

I got hold of Nadia Lutfi's phone number with the help of a friend, the journalist Mohamed Shoair, but it took me a year to summon up the courage to call her, which I eventually did from Canada on September 14, 2014. What prompted me to make the call was an interview, "Nadia Lutfi Tells the Secret of Enayat al-Zayyat's Suicide," which was published by *al-Musawwar* magazine on May 16, 1967—less than two months after the publication of Enayat's novel.

In his introduction, the interviewer Foumil Labib writes:

Nadia Lutfi was keeper of secrets for the woman who wrote Love and Silence, *so it is she who best understands the full extent of the tragedy of that pen which was snapped before it could write down everything it had to say.*

Nadia talks about their first encounter:

The face of Enayat al-Zayyat never leaves my thoughts. If she ever leaves my thoughts I can summon her back in seconds. Enayat was a friend from early childhood. I met her at school. From the very first, there were differences. She was self-contained, carried her books with her everywhere, and loathed the shouting, squabbling girls whose leader I was. But when we moved up a year I sat next to her in class and discovered that she loved to draw, just like me. She was good at German, too, which meant I could cheat off her. We brought our friendship home from school. My family lived in Saad Zaghloul Mausoleum Street, and she was close by in Mounira. I was an only child and she became a sister to me, completed me. She was the second of three girls. Of course, her older sister was horrible to her, and she (of course) persecuted her younger sister, and then her older and younger sisters joined forces to encircle her. So she became friends with me: an alliance to counterbalance her sisters'.

They would do their homework together, says Nadia; they would go to the cinema. She says that she'd nagged Abbas al-Zayyat to let the two families spend their summer holidays together and that he'd agreed. She says that though she left the German School in 1953 to go to an Arabic-language school, Enayat stayed on. That they continued to meet after school.

In 1954, Nadia got married and went to live in Alexandria. Enayat grew tired of school and in 1956 she got married herself. Nadia says that when she was offered the chance to work in cinema she had gone to tell Enayat and her husband, and that the husband's acceptance of Nadia's career had delighted her, because she'd worried that he might come between them.

She makes a reference to Enayat giving up painting—*that pursuit which no longer engaged all her faculties*—and devoting herself to writing. She says that Enayat began to experience difficulties with her husband and regretted abandoning her studies to get married. That she was starting to run, trying to catch the last carriage of the train before it left the platform.

She was trying to catch up before it could pass her by, Nadia says, and she did this by continuing to study German, then getting a job at the German Archaeological Institute in Zamalek. She says that following her divorce, Enayat had come face-to-face with harsh reality, and that she, Nadia, had never spoken of this before:

I felt as though a fracture was spreading through her life. Enayat had always held fast to unbelievably pure ideals, and her conscience didn't let her make light of any break with them, whether it was her failure or someone else's. She went out to meet life and ran smack into it. Men weren't the way her kindhearted father had led her to believe and she was horrified to find that the world was a jungle, that there were some women who would mock anyone or anything in order to make it. It horrified her to find her sisters, her fellow women, so contemptuous of conscience and the soul. [. . .] That her son was in a tug-of-war between her and her husband only complicated things.

Nadia can't remember the names of the writers who read drafts of *Love and Silence*, but she says that a good number of them were impressed and encouraged Enayat. She says that Enayat submitted it to the publisher, that the publisher took forever getting back to her, and that she was overcome by anxiety.

Then the end, on January 3, 1964, while Nadia was celebrating her birthday in Alexandria: Enayat's phone call to say that she wouldn't be coming and that the publisher had got back to say the novel wasn't fit for publication. Nadia spent the night feeling resentful because this was the first time Enayat had missed her birthday. Early the next morning Nadia had flown down to Cairo, then what happened had happened, and Nadia had broken down.

The interview concludes with a list of the things that in Nadia's view could have driven Enayat to suicide:

I found out that a few days before she killed herself, she had received a message saying that her son was now at the age at which he had to leave her custody and go to live with the father. The darkness around her had grown darker: first her marriage had foundered, and now they were taking her only child, her hope and her joy. The breath she breathed through her book, they were choking it off, and the world was just strolling on by, indifferent.

Where was Enayat's son now, I wondered? Was there perhaps some way I could talk to him? I wanted to hear from Nadia about what Enayat had been reading. How and where had she written her novel? When had she finished it? What kind of life had she led after getting divorced and starting work? And there was that discrepancy in the dates: Nadia had her committing suicide in 1964, while Anis Mansour said 1963.

I'll check with her when we speak, I told myself.

But the most exciting thing in Nadia's interview wasn't any of this. It was the inclusion of two short texts by Enayat: paragraphs excerpted from her journal.

After the first of these, Foumil Labib interjects:

Having returned Enayat's scattered pages to the briefcase full of memories which contained her photographs and paintings, Nadia resumed . . .

Did this mean that, in 1967, Nadia Lutfi had owned a case full of Enayat's papers, photographs, and paintings?

I jotted down a few sentences, notes of what I wanted to say to whoever answered the phone. For some reason, I imagined that there would be some intermediary involved, but as it happened I forgot all my preparations because it was Nadia Lutfi herself who picked up.

I introduced myself (I was Egyptian, I said, then gave my academic title and explained that I was researching Enayat al-Zayyat) and immediately Nadia Lutfi began to talk. And so openly, too: as though she'd been discussing Enayat with a friend and I'd wandered up in the middle of the conversation. To my delight she started her story where it ended: her birthday party in Alexandria on January 3, 1963, and Enayat's phone call, then finding the body on the morning of January 5. This must be how it is to lose a friend: the actual moment of loss remains present in all its fine detail, a fixed point from which everything that precedes it can be recalled again and again.

- That's my sweetheart: my friend and my sister. You've no idea what her death did to me. For years I'd write her these letters, tell her everything that was going on in my life. To this day, she's still my one true friend; nobody's taken her place.

- We were together at the German School in Bab al-Louq. I was ten or eleven and she was a year older. I didn't like her at first. She used to sit in the playground reading. Didn't join in. I was naughty. I liked games and music and athletics, and I was a leader. In our second year there we ended up in the same class because she hadn't taken the exam to move up a year. She was the first person who got me to enjoy reading. But she only read German. In 1949, or maybe 1950, we read Youssef al-Sebaie's novel *I Am Going Away*. It was the first book she'd ever read in Arabic and we wept in each other's arms. After that, she started to read more Arabic. She adored Yehia Haqqi. We'd go and buy books from Madbouli's back when it was a pavement stall, then we'd pretend we were older than we were and go and sit in Groppi's. We were just fourteen.

- I was an only child. Papa and Mama were extremely conservative and protective. I was being smothered. Her father was Abbas al-Zayyat. I'd never met anyone like him. He was completely different to the other fathers. Like, he was friends with his daughters, and Enayat in particular. He'd take them to the cinema and the theater and he had this huge library in the apartment itself. There were three girls—Aida, the eldest, then Enayat, then Azima—and they all went to the same school in Bab al-Louq. I became Enayat's sister. Whenever Faten Hamama had a new film out, Abbas would take us to see it together.

- No, she wasn't close to her mother at all. Her mother was

from a Turkish family. Highly strung and not friendly with her daughters. Very pretty, though. She'd been raised like a princess. Spoiled. But she wasn't close to Enayat.

- We used to go up to Alexandria for the summer, and Enayat's family would take their holidays in Ras al-Barr. After she and I became friends, we started going to Ras al-Barr, too, so we could be together, and sometimes we managed to persuade Uncle Abbas to come with us to Alexandria. Ras al-Barr was just beautiful: all bamboo and beach huts and swimming races. We used to set out together, all in a rush: from in front of the Savoy Hotel out to the lighthouse. I loved competing and Enayat loathed it. The only competition she'd take part in was memorizing phone numbers: Casino Courteille, 4; the Savoy, 7; the Lighthouse Hotel, 8; Hotel Aslan, 9—all the way through the fateer places and confectioners till she got to 166. We went to a Nagat al-Saghira concert together. Nagat was about our age and she sang songs by Umm Kulthoum, so we started listening to Umm Kulthoum. Before that we'd only ever listened to Leila Mourad. I have a lot of pictures of us from those trips. When you come, I'll show them to you. I've got a box of Enayat's photographs upstairs, next to the bed in the spare room.

- In Alexandria, I discovered that Enayat absolutely loved painting. And shoes. She once spent everything she had on a pair with bows by Georges Sara.

- Enayat was a quiet person but her mood could change like that. Sometimes she'd fight with her sisters then come round to mine to do her homework. She'd sleep over and end up fighting with me. If that happened, if war was declared, the only person she'd speak to was my Aunt Nana. Aunt Nana was not much older than us and she knew much better than anyone how to deal with Enayat when she was out of sorts. Later Nana went to America and ended up living there because her husband worked for Royal Bank.

- I declared revolution against the German School in 1953. That school was just terrifying: all rules and regulations. I went to an Arabic-language school instead. We'd meet every day after class, and it was around then that Enayat started giving up painting and the piano and began to write these anonymized sketches of people she knew.

- I married very young. I was out walking in Heliopolis near Ismailia Square when this beautiful black car pulls over and a handsome officer gets out. What's your name? he says. Like a fantasy, you know? I was terrified. He asked me for my address, and I gave it to him, then I went off to tell Aunt Nana and Enayat what had happened. The officer came round to the house—Adel al-Beshari, a navy man— and he brought his father with him: Brig. Abdel Fattah al-Beshari, commander of the Egyptian forces in Sudan and a personal friend of President Mohamed Naguib. So Mohamed Naguib and Enayat were both at my wedding. I was living between Cairo and Alexandria at the time. In 1956, Adel was in the navy, his brother was in the air force, his first brother-in-law was in the army, and his second brother-in-law was a pilot. All the men in that family were at war, in other words, and all the women would sit around in my mother-in-law's house in Heliopolis, following the news on the radio. It was during that time that Enayat and I started seeing each other every day again.

- She dropped out of school in 1955, just before her baccalaureate exams, and got married that same year. Or maybe that was in 1956. I had my boy and she had hers a year later. I was working in cinema and she was focused on writing. Cinema and literature: like we were always on the same path, you know?

I heard a woman's voice telling Nadia that she had a call on her mobile, then Nadia in reply, protesting that she was busy with an important call from Canada. Then Nadia was talking to me again, asking if I minded that she take the other call. She was gone five minutes and while she was away I realized that our conversation had already lasted an hour, that for a whole hour I had been panting and scribbling and listening to my heart pound. My neck was aching from the weight of the receiver and I switched over to the speaker and tried to find myself a better pen. *In our second year there we ended up in the same class because she hadn't taken the exam.* I underlined this because I wanted to ask why an excellent student like Enayat would miss her exams. I thought about how Nadia and Enayat's stories were intertwined, how difficult it would be to unpick one from the other.

Then Nadia was back:

"So, what were we saying? Enayat got married to Kamal Shaheen of the Shaheen Soap family. He was a pilot, and wealthy, but he wasn't like us: he hadn't gone to a foreign-language school and he didn't like books or films. She was naïve and she was young and he was a rough man. One night during Ramadan, she called me up and Adel and I went round to their place. Her husband was away, so we stayed up with her, then stayed over. That was the night she told us she wanted a divorce. Wasn't prepared to listen to anything we had to say. She had this hardness. And she was a revolutionary, too. Well it was a time of transition, wasn't it? We were all revolutionaries. Enayat and I, we were pioneers. We knew that the social changes taking place were no joke and that our generation was capable of doing anything it wanted to."

I recalled that Nadia had used the world *transition* in her interview with Foumil Labib, and I wanted to ask her just what she meant by that, but chose not to interrupt the flow.

"We both had children, but when I started working in cinema I gave my boy to Mama to raise and I'd go to see them in Alexandria whenever I had time to spare. In Cairo, I'd stay with my sister-in-law, Sousou, in Garden City. Later on, I bought my own apartment right next door. Ustaz Abbas had left Mounira by that time and built himself a beautiful two-story villa in Dokki. I can still remember the exact address: No. 16, Abdel Fattah al-Zeini Street.

"Enayat's problems with her husband got worse and she asked for a divorce and went to live with her father. She insisted on living alone. Uncle Abbas was an understanding man. When he saw that she meant it, he didn't attempt to persuade her to try again. He gave her the flat above his so that she could be independent. There were lots of court cases between her and her husband, first because of the divorce, then over custody. She was terrified he would take the boy from her when he reached seven.

"You see, depression's a predisposition, an illness, and that predisposition was in her. The battle with her husband over her son played a role in her depression, but so did the writing. There was frustration because of the writing.

"I often wonder about our differences. We were like a single bean split in two, sure, but after the split, her half shut up shop. Me, I talk and I laugh and I shout, but she wasn't like that. I've got this thing where, when I get into difficulties, I turn them into comedy. When I'm in crisis, I laugh. I think that might be the difference. When Enayat was in pain, when she was suffering, she didn't know how to say so. It took her a long time to talk."

I judged that the moment had come to ask Nadia about Enayat's reading habits and how she'd learned Arabic. When, exactly, had she finished the novel, and why had she taken it to writers like Mustafa Mahmoud, Anis Mansour, and Youssef al-Sebaie? Why them in particular? But as with Shahrazad, dawn came at last. I heard the voices of guests and Nadia greeting them. I thanked her from my heart. "Call me any time in the evening," she said sweetly, then added something that deeply affected me: "It's Enayat who brought you to me. She wants me to tell you about her."

My conversations with Nadia continued all the way through the autumn of 2014. She wasn't always in the same gregarious mood as on our first call. Sometimes I would sense that she didn't want to talk and would make do with hellos. At other times, her desire to speak would astonish me: as soon as she heard my voice on the line she was talking. "I just remembered something. So glad you've called . . ." There were times she would welcome my questions and times she would become irritated if I said something she didn't care for. For instance, when I asked her if Enayat had read *The Open Door* or had been influenced by Latifa al-Zayyat when she wrote *Love and Silence*, she said firmly, "You're not right about that at all. Latifa al-Zayyat? Latifa was one thing and Enayat was something else. Enayat had finished her book before Latifa's novel came out. Enayat and I were a different generation entirely. Revolutionary, sure, but our revolution was different to Latifa's. You can lump Latifa in with the political activists, but you can't do the same with Enayat. Enayat had a German-language background. She learned Arabic in order to write. She was constantly fretting. She didn't believe in anything at all. It's as simple as that. We were the transition generation: all hunger and energy."

I began looking forward to these calls avidly. Hearing her voice made me feel very close to Enayat. Occasionally, I would have problems picturing a friendship like theirs. I myself had never had the good fortune to live in such intimate proximity with another woman. Her fickle moods made me respect her more. I never trust the even-tempered. I'd ask myself: with a mind so alive, with a memory so strong and so precise and a life lived to its fullest, why doesn't she write her memoirs? I wished there could be a second me to trace her story, too, but then again—or so I supposed—her story was destined to be a part of Enayat's.

On page 42 of *Love and Silence* is a passage in which Najla describes her friendship with Nadia. I took it as a message to me from Enayat:

I sat back and listened to Nadia as she broke our friendship down into words, and as she did this she seemed far away from me. The qualities she named weren't those on which the foundations of our affection were built, I thought, but then again, whenever we try to translate feelings into words we rob them of much of their depth. What lay between myself and Nadia was not so easily described.

I set myself to reread *Love and Silence*. What exactly changed in this reading I couldn't say, but it wasn't innocent anymore. I was trying to imagine Enayat, twenty-two or twenty-three years old, mother of a child she was terrified of losing to his father, returning home each night from the German Institute in Zamalek to her father's building in Dokki, climbing the stairs to her flat, then working on the book while her young son slept. I tried to imagine her sleepless, torn between the demands of the divorce and custody battles and the desire to write, and all the while waiting and waiting for al-Qawmiyya to reply.

6.

Law 270, issued on November 10, 1952, prescribes the creation of a Ministry of National Guidance, with the following aims:

1. Directing and guiding members of the umma towards that which will elevate them materially and morally, strengthen their resolve and sense of responsibility, and motivate them to be cooperative and selfless and to redouble their efforts in the service of the homeland, giving them necessary instruction in how to combat epidemics, crop disease, and harmful habits, and, in general, promoting all things that might assist in making good citizens of them.

2. Making popular culture accessible to all members of the population, diversifying and supporting it in order to extend its reach and to benefit the greatest possible number of people.

3. Presenting the results of civic and governmental efforts to marshal and guide public opinion both locally and

internationally, showcasing those projects which are either completed or in the planning stage, in fields of the arts, the sciences, and urban development.

Around the same time, an initiative called the Thousand Book Project was taking root and flourishing. The idea was to use the money budgeted for school libraries to print books in all fields—the sciences, literature, and the arts—under the aegis of the Ministry of Education. Privately owned publishing houses were given funds to print the books, which were then distributed to school libraries and other institutions. It was commonplace to find translations of canonical works of Western literature alongside Arabic literature and textbooks on relativity, Coptic history, and the monuments of Ancient Egypt.

One of the jobs of the Ministry of National Guidance was to churn out propaganda. Take, for instance, *Our Struggle Against the Invaders*, which was published following the Tripartite Aggression in 1956. Jointly written by a group of history professors, each assigned a chapter describing a different foreign invasion of Egypt along with an account of local resistance at that time, it ran through various Pharaonic periods such as the Hyksos, and on to the Crusader armies fought off by the Arabs; it concluded with the creation of Israel. There were series which contained transcripts of radio broadcasts by famous writers, and more, including the *People's Court* series, the *Revolutionary Court* series, and the *Presidents' Speeches* series which carried on until 1959.

It was a time of proliferating cultural institutions and strong governmental interventions in the processes of cultural production. In 1956, the Supreme Council for the Supervision of the Arts and Literatures was established: an independent body under the direction of the cabinet which sought to coordinate the efforts of government and civil society. Another significant development took place on June 25, 1958, when by presidential decree the Ministry of National Guidance was reorganized and Fathy Radwan appointed minister. One day later, a second decree was issued, renaming it the Ministry of Culture and National Guidance. Radwan remained as minister for a few months, and then in October of the same year Tharwat Okasha was recalled from Italy to replace him, a position he retained until 1962. This was the period in which Enayat submitted her novel to al-Qawmiyya. Okasha returned to his post in September 1966, and held it until November 1970, and it was in this period that Enayat's novel was rediscovered and published.

In March 1959, Okasha issued invitations to a convention at the Opera House, where a series of meetings, debates, and subcommittees was held to hear the concerns and priorities of Egyptian intellectuals, after which the heavy industrialization of culture began in earnest. Okasha immediately drew up plans to build museums and galleries, as well as founding a printing and publishing house with a budget of 250,000 Egyptian pounds. This was al-Qawmiyya. In just one year, state publishing became a powerful sector of its own, served by several printer-publishers as well as al-Taleef wal Targama, a separate imprint for Arabic-language novels and translations.

It is difficult to imagine that Enayat was at all aware of these developments, either as a student at the German School in 1955, or as a married woman from 1956, or after she left her marital home and was fighting her divorce case through the courts. But after completing her novel in May 1960 she began her search for a publisher, and from this point on, her fate would be intertwined with the fortunes of the Nasserist cultural machine. Even after her death.

In the summer of 1960, a twenty-four-year-old Enayat was living in Dokki, in the building owned by her father, Abbas al-Zayyat, tracking the progress of her divorce case through the courts and passing pencil-written drafts of her novel to writer acquaintances of the actress Nadia Lutfi, in the hope that one of them might be able to get it published or write an introduction. Her father suggested she self-publish but she rejected the idea out of hand. Her dream was to see *Love and Silence* accepted by a recognized publisher.

Enayat wrote out a list of the authors and publishers that she had heard of. She began with writers whose books she'd read but whom she had never met: Yehia Haqqi, her favourite, used a variety of publishers, including the Ministry of Culture and Guidance, the General Egyptian Institute for Publishing, Dar al-Maaref, and the al-Majalla al-Jadida Press; Naguib Mahfouz brought all his books out with Misr Press; Ihsan Abdel Quddous worked with al-Khanji or Dar al-Fikr al-Arabi.

As for the writers she had met in person through Nadia, Mustafa Mahmoud and Anis Mansour were with Dar al-Maaref, and Youssef al-Sebaie with al-Khanji and Misr Press. The author of *The Open Door*, released just a month earlier, used Anglo Press. Her father told her that Mahmoud Taymour, her mother's uncle and a man she had only ever seen at family functions, published with a press called al-Adaab in Gamameez Lane. In the end, it seems, Enayat managed to persuade herself that the Ministry of Culture and Guidance was supportive of the new generation, and that al-Qawmiyya was committed to the cultural revolution that Gamal Abdel Nasser had called for.

One January morning in 1961, father and daughter went together to the offices of al-Qawmiyya with a copy of the novel which Enayat had typed up herself on an Optima. She signed the submissions ledger and wrote her phone number next to her name, receiving in exchange a receipt that bore her name, the title of the novel, and the date of submission. On the back of the receipt she jotted down the name and number of al-Qawmiyya's secretary—*Lola Saad (40850)*—with a note to herself to expect a reply within a fortnight.

No call came. When Enayat called Lola Saad, the secretary told her to wait until Ramadan and Eid were over. Eid al-Fitr fell on March 19, Eid al-Adha on May 20, and then there was July Revolution Day. Each time she would wait till the holiday was over and then, every evening after she got home from work, the same question: "Did anyone call?"

In August 1961, Enayat wrote the following in her journal:

Anxiety, come, enfold me, and cast off this choking lifelessness. Smear your bitterness across my lips, dye my world with your bitterness, but don't leave me in this lethargy. Come. I am a lost soul in search of color. Life runs on without me and I am left lifeless,

homeless, more absent than not. The curtains are drawn and the
lamps are lit in the buildings opposite. The people there feel warm
and safe, whereas I, I have no home, no roof, no walls.

In the autumn of 1962, Enayat visited the publisher's
offices to ask what had happened to the novel she'd submitted
more than a year before. Lola Saad, the secretary, wasn't there,
and by then Tharwat Okasha had been replaced by Abdel
Kader Hatem, whose brief had been expanded to include
tourism, media, and antiquities. It is impossible to know if
Enayat was aware of these momentous structural changes, but
an employee at al-Qawmiyya told her that she would have to
wait a few months more, because the publisher was midway
through implementing changes in its strategy.

It appears that Enayat closely followed al-Qawmiyya's
latest releases, as though knowing the type of books they were
publishing would somehow tell her when her novel would
have its day. Her heart would pound every time she saw the
lists of new titles, each barely distinguishable from the next.
Things like *The Socialism of Islam* (Mustafa al-Sebaie, 1960),
The Mother of Socialism: Khadija bint Khuwaylid (Ibrahim Zaki
al-Saie, 1960), or *Islam: Religion and Socialism* (Ahmed Faraag,
1961). On this second visit to the publisher she picked up one
of these volumes, tickled not only by the verbosity of the
title (*Cooperative Democratic Socialist Philosophy: A Study from
the Perspective of Arab Nationalism, Arab Society, and the Current
System of Government*, 1961) but also at the length of the
author's name: one Ahmed Ezz al-Din Abdallah Khalfallah.

That same day she bought several books, including
Sacrifices in the Talmud and Ibn Battuta's *Travels*, the latter

because she had seen an old copy in the library of the German Archaeological Institute. Then an Arabic translation by Omar Abdel Aziz Amin of *Die Leiden des jungen Werthers*, a book she'd first read in German, and in fact the only book whose many errors and infelicities (starting with the title, which the translator rendered as *Werther: A Tragic Romance*) she saw fit to mark and comment on. At first, she seems to have derived considerable pleasure from comparing the Arabic to the original, but about thirty pages in she grew bored of the exercise and stopped.

Fortunately, Enayat was in the habit of marking the first page of each of her books with the date and place she'd bought it. After her death, *Werther: A Tragic Romance* was relocated, along with some other books, from her apartment in Dokki to that of her sister, Aida, in Zamalek, and from there to a relative's home in Heliopolis, which is where I found myself one evening in the summer of 2015, poring through the notes that cluttered the margins.

7.

The first time we spoke, I hadn't had the chance to ask about Enayat's surviving family. It was during our second conversation that Nadia told me she had only stayed in touch with one of them, Enayat's father, and that she had last seen him in 1967 when he had come round to her flat in Garden City with a copy of *Love and Silence*, which had just been released. He'd been so overcome he'd wept, she said, and had thanked her for her role in getting the book published. She told me that her relationship with Enayat's sisters hadn't ever been a strong one, but she believed Aida had passed away some years ago. She had no idea how to find Azima, because "she used to live abroad with her husband the diplomat."

"Look here," she said. "The truth is that I was her only sister and she was mine. When you come and see me I'll show you the note she wrote to me once. *To Nadia, my true sister.* It's in the box by the bed in the guest room. I've never known anybody who has even come close to the place I hold for Enayat. My whole life, I've cared about one thing and one thing only, and that's friendship. I was raised a single child and

I was given too much attention. Smothered, when all I wanted was friendship and freedom. Whether in my relationships or my career, I've always been able to break ties without ever breaking myself—but Enayat's death did break me. Let me ask you then, since you're the one on her trail: explain to me why she committed suicide. Tell me and I'll listen."

I was certain that Nadia had been closer than anybody to Enayat—friends are always the closest—but I also wanted to see Enayat through her family's eyes. I drew a red line beneath Azima al-Zayyat's name. I should look for her.

It was March 8, 2015, at home in Canada, when it occurred to me that the best way to get in touch with surviving members of al-Zayyat's family might be to search through newspaper obituaries online. A search of Aida al-Zayyat's name led me to the obituary of her husband, Anwar Abdel Karim Habb al-Rouman, described as a former director of the Military Academy and *father of Mohammed Anwar and Ibrahim Anwar*. The obituary, dated May 16, 2002, contained no other information about the two sons, such as their professions, that I could use to track them down. But that surname: Habb al-Rouman. Pomegranate seed! Strange and beautiful and distinctive. Where had I seen it before? I entered it into Google: *Colonel Habb al-Rouman*. There he was, referenced in a book about heroes of the October War of 1973: promoted to command of the Sixteenth Division, part of the Second Field Army, after its original commander, Brig. Gen. Abd Rabbennabi Hafez was injured by shrapnel from an Israeli artillery bombardment on October 18, 1973, during the engagement known as the Battle of the Chinese Farm. An hour passed, as I read now about Abd Rabbennabi and now about the battle, and then I realized that I had forgotten what I was supposed to be doing, and was disappointed with myself.

I typed in *Azima al-Zayyat* and pulled up another obituary, this time from *al-Ahram*:

Verily we are from Allah and to Him we return.

His Excellency, Ambassador Mohammed Hussein Saeed al-Sadr, has passed on into the Mercy of Almighty Allah, eldest son of the artist and former director of the College of Applied Arts, Saeed al-Sadr, and the late Mrs. Doriya al-Sadr; husband of Mrs. Azima Abbas al-Zayyat, and father to two children, engineer Hossam al-Inbabi and Mrs. Iman al-Sadr, a teacher at the Collège de la Mère de Dieu . . .

Amid the branching tangle of al-Sadrs, I found what I was looking for: *and brother-in-law to the late Mrs. Aida al-Zayyat and the late author Mrs. Enayat al-Zayyat.*

Reading this last line I almost trilled out a zaghrouta. The most promising lead here was a name: Iman al-Sadr. I looked up her email address at the Collège de la Mère de Dieu and her Facebook account and wrote to her: a brief introduction to myself and my research, and my hope that she might reply.

I remembered a book I'd read more than two decades ago: *Saeed al-Sadr, Magician of Time.* It had been given to me by its author, Mokhtar al-Attar, in about 1995. I'd gone to his apartment in downtown Cairo in the company of my old friend, Abdel Moneim Saoudi, "the last communist," as we called him: a man who'd spent a decade of his life in Abdel Nasser's prisons. My friendship with Saoudi dated from five years earlier: he had been working at al-Ghad, which had published my first collection of poetry. In 1993, I bought a flat in Faisal, and he gifted me the entire archive of HADITU, or the Democratic Movement for National Liberation, which was the main Egyptian communist organization of the late 1940s and early 1950s. "I've moved these documents between many homes," he had said, "but now I don't have anywhere to live and I want you to look after them."

I started meeting up with Saoudi and his old comrades, sessions where they'd swap memories of events we had only read about. Laughter often, sometimes tears. I would interview them and dream of writing about them. The archive, the interviews, *Saeed al-Sadr, Magician of Time*—everything from this period of my life must still be lying in dust-caked boxes up in the attic of my father's house, and some day soon, if they hadn't already, somebody was going to decide it was worthless junk and throw it away.

At six o'clock on the morning of March 10, I saw Iman al-Sadr's reply: *My dear Iman Mersal, Sorry my Arabic is so poor. I'm so happy that you know Enayat al-Zayyat. She was my aunt, and I have some pictures of her. If you want, I can send them to you. Thank you so much for your interest. I always wished I could have met my aunt.*

For an hour we typed back and forth in English. She told me that I should speak to Nadia Lutfi, and I told her that I had been in touch with Nadia since the previous autumn, and that I had traveled to Cairo in February in order to meet her and had failed.

I said that I had failed to locate Abbas al-Zayyat's file at Cairo University, and I'd failed to trace the street in Dokki where Enayat had lived. Iman sent me a number of photographs of Enayat's face, and others of her with various family members, none of whom I was able to identify with any certainty. Then she sent a phone number, a landline, and said that if I wanted to speak to her mother, Azima al-Zayyat, I could call right away. I replied that I would call the number in an hour once my son was at school, because my husband was traveling with my youngest and I was alone at home.

I let Mourad walk to school, despite public warnings about ice on the road.

From the outset I could sense Azima's eagerness to talk to me, but there was a bitterness there, too, a resentment that Enayat had been forgotten. She asked me if I was going to reissue the novel and I told her that of course I wanted to, but made it clear that I had no direct control over anything like that—only that my writing about Enayat might encourage a publisher to do so. She told me that a film had been made based on the novel and that it was terrible, and I said that I'd seen it: that in my opinion it was a ridiculous film and the only thing it took from the book was the title. The one scene I could remember was the actress Nelly pretending to weep over the death of Hisham, while standing in front of a mirror gluing quarter-kilo eyelashes to her face.

Azima didn't laugh.

My attention was focused on the way Azima told her story. I only wrote down those things that Nadia had omitted from her account, or when the details differed, or to make a record of the language she used. From Azima, I learned that her father, Abbas, was from the Mansoura branch of the al-Zayyats, though none of his daughters had ever been to Mansoura. Their connection to the father's side of the family was confined to those relatives who lived in Cairo, like her two paternal aunts, one of whom was mother of the poet and journalist Mustafa Bahgat Badawi, while the other married into the al-Baz family. Her mother, Fahima Ali Abbas, was daughter of Zeinab, granddaughter of Rashid Pasha, who had been a minister more than once in the administration of Khedive Ismail. Fahima's father was Turkish, born in Egypt. The neighborhoods around Mounira—Abdeen Palace and Saad Zaghloul's Mausoleum—had teemed with Rashid Pasha's descendants in the 1940s, but in the wake of the July Revolution these neighborhoods had grown crowded and the family had departed, some to Heliopolis, others to Maadi, while Abbas had bought himself a plot of land in Dokki, building a house for himself and moving there in about 1957.

I asked Azima if she knew the address of the building in Dokki or the location of Rashid Pasha's tomb, and for the first time, the atmosphere grew strained.

"What do you want addresses for?" she said. "What have they got to do with anything?"

To ease the tension, I changed the subject, and asked when she and her sisters had been born.

"Aida was born in 1934, Enayat in 1936, and I came along in 1938. My father was an admirer of German education, so he sent us to the German School in Bab al-Louq. It was strict, run by nuns. One after another, at two-year intervals, we all got married. Aida was working as a secretary at the Swiss Antiquities Institute in Zamalek and lived just round the corner. She passed away in 2012. Her husband, Anwar Abdel Karim Habb al-Rouman, was like a brother to us. He died before her, may God have mercy on him."

When I asked how Enayat had started writing, she said that she'd written stories in German from a very young age, and had won prizes for writing and drawing at school. "From very young, she was always asking about life and death. Papa started reading what she wrote in Arabic when she was around thirteen or fourteen. Before they built over it, the German School had this big playground, and she used to sit there reading. Everything was taught in German except minor subjects like Arabic and French. All Enayat ever wanted to be was a writer."

Nadia Lutfi's name came up several times. In Azima's view, "Nadia and Papa were the two people closest to Enayat," and she advised me to ask Nadia any question that she herself was unable to answer.

I can't remember when I became conscious of it, but the strained note that first entered her voice when I'd asked for the addresses had now returned, and was growing more pronounced the longer the conversation went on. There was a defensiveness in response to questions that contained no trace of accusation, like when I asked her which year Enayat had married and she said, "She didn't go to university. She wasn't even nineteen when she got married. I went to the American University for a couple of years but I didn't finish. It was normal for a girl to marry young."

When I asked her for the name of Enayat's husband, and whether he had really been a pilot and the son of Mohammed Shaheen, owner of Shaheen's Nabulsi Soaps, as Nadia had claimed, Azima politely demurred. It was "old news," she said. "The man himself is dead and there's no call for me to bring his name into it. He was a pilot in the air force and he wasn't like us. They separated about two or three years into the marriage. The divorce took ages. He was from a big family, and now he's dead, and there's no point bringing it up. Are you writing about Enayat or her husband?"

When it came to Abbas, Enayat's child, Azima spoke at length:

"Her son was just about starting to walk when her husband took him away from her. A very sad business. So many problems. I can't remember if she was allowed to see the child or not. The boy used to go and see his father and he'd come back turned against her. You're not my mama, he'd say. I was there this one time and he called her Auntie. Mama is what he called his father's new wife. The father and his wife were making him behave like that."

I noticed that Azima would talk about "Enayat's passing" but never once used the word suicide, and though I was on the verge of putting it to her, I decided it would be too painful. Instead, I asked her the question that had been on my mind since we'd started talking. Could she put me in touch with Enayat's son? Maybe she could talk to him about my project and see if he'd be prepared to meet me when I visited Egypt in the summer. The silence dragged out for almost a minute, then Azima said, "Abbas died in 1983, in the prime of his youth."

My hands, quite literally, began to shake. Any desire I had to know more evaporated. There are things that always deserve silence, but I had to force that heavy weather aside and end the conversation on a gentler note. Azima must be suffering. Who knows what grief and pain she had endured and come through in the wake of her sister's death?

I'd read somewhere that every suicide leaves a minimum of six people to deal with the trauma of accepting and understanding what has happened. They are usually family or friends, though the circle of those affected can extend to include colleagues and neighbors. Suicide is not simply a death: its wake is dyed with guilt and shame and a confusion over how to establish responsibility for, or minimize, its impact. How many times had Nadia said, "Maybe if I'd been by her side on January 3, 1963, if I'd been able to console her, it never would have happened"?

I went out. Not a soul in the street and one below zero felt positively warm after the long winter. But still below zero: the snow clung on in slippery patches, mirrored sheets that could unbalance anyone who crossed them. As I walked, picking my way between the mirrors, I thought about what had happened to Abbas. He'd been six when Enayat had died. Had they ever shown him the note that Enayat had left? *I do love you, it's just that life is unbearable. Forgive me.* I couldn't ask Azima a question like that. I had wanted to ask Abbas if he remembered refusing to call her Mama. If he had remembered, then he surely would have hated his father for it, would have hated himself. A true orphan.

1983! So he had died at roughly the same age as his mother. Was it as simple as inheriting her depression and misfortune, or was it just coincidence: two quite different fates that fell out along the same lines?

I got home to find several missed calls from Mourad's school, and when I called them back, was told that he'd slipped on the ice and injured his leg. The school nurse was looking after him, but the cut would need treatment at the hospital.

As the surgeon tied off the last of the eight stitches in Mourad's knee I was feeling furious. A great rage at myself.

Between my first conversation with Azima al-Zayyat in March and May 24, when we next spoke, I was writing a piece entitled "On Motherhood and Violence" for *Makhzin* magazine. It started as a brief, academic overview of the status of motherhood in some Western feminist discourses, but the theoretical questions raised led me to my own experience with motherhood and its guilt, terror, selfishness, and conflict. And although I was completely absorbed in this project, Enayat never left my mind. It was as though she was keeping me company, and in a new light.

I reread the novel and the published extracts from her journal.

In the novel, Najla pays a visit to her cousin, Sharifa, to congratulate her on the birth of her daughter. Najla wonders:

How is it that for all of human history, women have been men's possessions, less than them, even though they give them life and mother us all? Why don't the devastating agonies that sweep their bodies as they bear each new child into the world cause men to be kind to them, or tender?

Questions that must have preoccupied Enayat when she became a mother herself, as she returned to her father's house in Dokki, leaving her marital home behind and holding in her arms a child on the verge of walking.

I pictured Abbas asleep at her side as she wrote:

Woman is content with her role as mother and life-giver, and thinks little of the years lost raising children: a lifetime lost to a life without work. As she comes face-to-face with the newborn, work fades to nothing. But am I the same as Sharifa? Just a mother who conceives and labors and births, gladly building new generations with her offspring? Impossible. I want to work.

But the work Najla wants is generative too: she wants to give to the world something new and of herself. She decides to return to drawing, to submit her portfolio to the College of Fine Arts. As though the angst felt by the childless Najla contains something of Enayat's inner conflict between her love for her son and her desire to catch the last carriage of that departing train: to take a job at the German Archaeological Institute and write the novel.

Enayat's relationship with Abbas did not exist in isolation from the complexities of her life: a woman of twenty-three or twenty-four, mother, writer, and divorcée, with a son who spent half his time with her and half with his father. A son who would return to her arms freighted with love and damage. It must have hurt her deeply when he refused to call her Mama.

In one of the journal extracts, she writes:

We own no one and no one owns us.

Life changes, people change, nothing stays the same.
Even children . . .
Who took shape within us and fed on our blood.
Whose price was the terrible agonies of labor.
Even that child who inherited some of my nature,
whose features are my own.
Even him, whose smile is my smile,
whose little toe is bent, like mine.
Even him, whom I fed with my milk, my love.
Even him, for whom I stayed awake so he might sleep.
Even he changes.
Even he forgets me.
He has seen nothing of life.
He is still on the shore.
What will he do when he finds himself in it up to his knees?
Will he be lost to me forever?

The anger is familiar. The hearts of the depressed fracture easily against those they love, even children, even those who *fed on our blood*, as Enayat wrote. She had loved him very much. She went to war against her ex-husband, a fighter pilot and scion of a powerful family, in order to keep custody of him. She rehearsed Abbas's loss each time he left her side and went to his father.

One night, Enayat wrote:

And the red doll with the bell has stopped his noise. Little Nounou, who would rock him in his cot, has gone away. They've all gone away, and the laughter has died, and the house is like a ribcage, missing a beating heart.

Its soul is fled.

Three months after speaking with Azima al-Zayyat, I was back in Cairo armed with texts to guide me in my dealings with the archive I was sure was there. There was a box by the bed in Nadia Lutfi's spare room, I told myself; there are boxes and boxes that Azima will open for me.

A dusty room, is how I imagined it. Windowless. A room where no one had set foot in fifty years and very small indeed: sleeping quarters for the nanny back when there were children about, or for the maid in the grand old days. Or maybe just a storeroom. What mattered was that there were boxes there and, inside them, the draft of *Love and Silence*, papers filled with scrawled meditations whose meaning I would struggle to unlock, pictures, negatives, and a handful of Enayat's pencil sketches. There'd be letters I would read then return to their envelopes. A stamp commemorating the eighth anniversary of the revolution; a second from the United Arab Republic. Somewhere here, of course, sat documents from the case she had spent years pursuing through the courts. Then the journal she'd kept since her days as a student at the German School, first between the rose-patterned paper covers of an exercise book, then in green, hard-backed Romney notebooks, then through the last years of her life in two or three ledgers, bought at a stationer's in Kamel Sidqi Street in Fagaala, with the years embossed in gold: *1961, 1962, 1963.* Just three pages filled out in the last of these, or maybe more—who knows? Maybe she spent her final hours writing. Also: old shopping lists tucked between the pages of her books, or, at the very least, a Georges Sara receipt from 1950s Alexandria, bearing the famous logo and beneath it, in English: *G. S.—since 1905.* Nadia had said she'd been there in 1956 when Enayat had bought the satin shoes for her wedding. Eight pounds they'd cost her. But then Nadia couldn't remember whether they'd been from Georges Sara as she'd originally claimed, or from Lumbroso.

How this mythical room came to occupy my imagination so completely, I've no idea. Enayat's personal archive was all I could think about. It was as though she had sorted and ordered it herself, as though it was sitting there in the dust and dark, waiting for the one who would come to claim it. There is, by the way, no clear definition of "personal archive" other than an archive which exists in opposition to the institutional, or collective, archive. It is not a documentary record of oneself but rather a narrative. Not, then, a disconnected assemblage of facts, or truths about that person, but a life's worth of needs and desires, dreams and illusions: a record of their mutual misunderstanding with the world.

Maybe I imagined that I would find what Sue McKemmish, in "Evidence of Me," terms *the complete personal archive*: what belongs to any writer whose life has intersected with enough events (and other writers) to generate documentable transformations and layers of experience, enough to accumulate significantly over time, enough so that, onion-like, it can later be peeled back and exposed. Conventionally, the importance of any given personal archive derives from the achievements of its subject or, say, their social and cultural status; it can even derive from the conflicts which arise between those who seek to impose their authority over what can be accessed and what is to be redacted in the personal archives of the dead.

All of which I chose to ignore, dreaming instead of my treasure, my trove of all things Enayat.

8.

A delicate white blouse was not the right choice for a search through Enayat's boxes. I thought of swapping it for something darker, hesitated, and, as I so often do when caught between alternatives, in the end chose both, folding a white shirt into my rucksack as a spare. On the way to the front door, I took a bottled water from the fridge, then paused, pulled a small recording device from my pocket, and pushed the button: "Hello . . . hello . . . hello there . . . Meeting with Mrs. Azima al-Zayyat, evening of July 15, 2015, Cairo."

Played back, my voice sounded faint. I tried again, making sure the thing was working: "Hello . . . hello . . . hi . . . This is my first meeting with Mrs. al-Zayyat at her home in Maadi, and the third time we've spoken following the two phone calls I made from Canada."

Though it was now half past eight in the evening, the heat and crowds in Roda Street came as a shock: the whole world was out, getting ready for Eid. Sheltered in the lee of two women, one with a young girl on her shoulders, I dodged the speeding cars and reached the pavement opposite.

Once in the taxi, feeling thirsty, I realized I had left the bottled water on the table.

At the home of Ambassador Hussein al-Sadr, I was met by Iman al-Sadr and her little Maltese, Vanilla. We had written to each other a number of times and had established a genuine rapport, but it was only as I stepped into their living room that the reality of Enayat's social background, something I hadn't considered much till now, struck me. There was old money here, present not only in a surface sheen of good taste, but also in a heavy, redolent atmosphere, its source perhaps the dense juxtaposition of disparate objects in the room: a pair of blue teacups that might have dated back to the monarchy, the furniture passed down through the generations and from home to home, keepsakes brought back by family members who'd lived overseas in South America, Africa, and Europe.

There were two watercolors by Saeed al-Sadr on the wall. He must have made them in the early 1970s, I thought, after he abandoned ceramics and returned to paint. There was also a large oil painting by Iman.

I recalled the confusion felt by the novel's protagonist, Najla, towards her own social class. The time she emerges from an exhibition with Ahmed, who, seeing a luxury car with its chauffeur patiently waiting, makes a comment about the idle rich and bloodsuckers, and she tells herself she never wants to own a car like that. I think about how embarrassed her revolutionary lover makes her feel towards her family's wealth, and that, although she knows he's right, she still makes an effort to accept her people, to reconcile with them: *I don't possess my wealth, I am only allowed the use of it. All I truly possess is my soul.*

Azima appeared. The conversation began with talk of the heat, of Ramadan and Eid, and I found Iman quietly taking my side, supporting me. She prompted her mother to bring out the papers and pictures that she'd found. My heart almost stopped. True, I had dreamed of being left by myself to open Enayat's boxes, of being allowed hours alone to look through them, but never mind. Azima produced an immaculate, evidently brand-new cardboard box, and took out a large number of family photographs and a few documents. I decided that if I took out my recorder it might spoil things, so I settled down to take notes as I listened to stories about the people in the pictures. I was cautious, too: careful not to inquire about Enayat's husband, or her relationship with her mother, or the divorce, or her suicide, or the death of her son, or the addresses of either the building in Dokki or the al-Afifi cemetery. But what did that leave? Relax, I told myself. Settle back, enjoy the hospitality, and get to know Azima. She was Enayat's sister after all; that was more than enough.

And strange to say, as if in response, Azima began to relax herself and to talk. She talked about her time at the German School and the domestic servant who used to draw up a daily menu for the three sisters in three separate columns, how Enayat had been withdrawn from a young age, about some of the girls she'd been friends with at the school. It suddenly struck me that I had never thought to visit the school and look up the names of her contemporaries.

*Enayat (far right) with her father, Abbas, her
mother, Fahima, and her sister Azima*

Then Iman went and fetched a pile of cassettes, recordings
of the serialization of *Love and Silence*. She had taken them
directly from the radio in the 1990s, she said, though it had
been first broadcast in the mid-1970s. Having hunted for
the tape player and turned it on, we were confronted by a
problem both simple and disconcerting: there were no credits
to give us the names of the director and writer and so on.
The distinctive voice of Mahmoud Morsi, playing the role of
Ahmed, was the only one we recognized.

I thought how strange it was that both a film and a radio
series could be adapted from a novel, while the novel itself
remained entirely absent from every history of twentieth-
century Egyptian and Arabic literature. Had Nadia Lutfi's
connections helped bring it to the attention of producers?

If so, then why hadn't she used the influence she'd certainly possessed by 1973 in order to ensure that the film was properly made? Maybe it had been nothing more than the general anarchy of the seventies, when production companies subsisted on written texts which they would cut and shape to fit their needs. So much was lost: only the most important serials and films from the period survived to live on in the public consciousness.

For the first time, Azima started to talk about Enayat's suicide, using the word. She said that on the evening of January 3, 1963, Enayat had left her son with her mother and said she was going out. That when she hadn't appeared the next morning, they had assumed she had gone to see Nadia, who must have come back to Cairo after her birthday party in Alexandria. That they'd waited for her until evening, then called Nadia. "Happy birthday," they had said. "Why's Enayat staying so late?" And Nadia had told them that she'd arrived back in Cairo early that morning. That she had waited for Enayat, and Enayat hadn't shown.

They went up to her flat. The bedroom door was locked so they peered through the glass pane. The bed seemed to be neatly made.

The next morning, the elder sister, Aida, came over from her flat in Zamalek and broke down the bedroom door. They found an empty box of Enayat's pink pills. And they found her.

Azima said despairingly, "We were so innocent, you see. We didn't know what depression was. These young people nowadays are more aware and they ask for help. We just didn't have that understanding, unfortunately."

Summoning my courage, I asked her why Enayat hadn't sat for her exams when she was twelve, despite her academic prowess. Was it because she was being treated for depression? "I don't know," Azima said.

In passing, she mentioned the name of the lawyer who'd represented Enayat during the divorce. As soon as I heard it, I realized that I knew his son: a lawyer himself, and a communist. I'd last seen him maybe two decades ago in his father's office, crammed with safes and papers. Where was the office again?

She came to Abbas, Enayat's only child. He had a degree in archaeology, Azima said. Married and died young. "How?" I couldn't hold the question in. "We don't know," she said. "We were in Egypt when it happened, a brief visit, and I went with Aida to the hospital. He lived in the same building as his father in Mohandiseen, a third-floor apartment. He'd gone out onto the balcony, waited until his father's car had pulled out into the street below, then fallen into the street."

Shyly, Iman interjected: "I saw him a few times at my Aunt Aida's. He had severe depression. We're not sure if it was an accident or suicide."

In the taxi on the way home, my heart was beating so fast that I felt overcome. Nerves and nausea. I tried to compose myself. Swapping the air conditioning for an open window didn't work, nor did the consideration of the driver, who switched off the radio and silenced a voice squawking on about the president and the vital importance of the new Suez Canal to Egypt's GNP. It was a panic attack. I asked the driver to drop me off anywhere along the Nile in Maadi.

"Anywhere?"
"Anywhere."

Enayat in the town of al-Qanatir
al-Khayriyyah, north of Cairo

I ended up overlooking the river in an approximation of a food court: a sprawling complex of restaurants and cafés thronged with families. People on their Ramadan fast were ordering pre-dawn meals and shisha pipes, and then there were the children, who in that moment seemed impossibly irritating to me, loathsome. I was so short of breath I wanted to scream. The waiter suggested I order pasta with calamari or a steak with mushrooms because there was a minimum charge.

I sat there sipping mint tea and gazing out at the Nile, the still sheet of its surface roiled and muddied by the noise around me. My mind was leaping all over. I thought about depression, about inheriting it: there was that boy who'd gone missing at university—two whole weeks without turning up for class and then we heard that he'd been found hanging from a tree. I thought about the communist lawyer and the zeal he showed during the demonstrations against the first Gulf War. Where was he now? Then came other faces, all the people I'd known and lost contact with since 1993. Suddenly, I remembered: the boxes slowly disappearing beneath the dust on my father's roof: my whole life before I left Egypt in 1998 being claimed by dust. Why had I never thought to sort through them and move the things that mattered to my flat in Manial? To avoid the pain it would cause, no doubt. I wondered about the difference between me and those people who easily dispose of the dead's possessions.

A boy in the tail of a pack of children bumped into me as he ran past. Madame Azima was right not to leave the house. In our conversation, when it became clear that she no longer went outside, I'd tried to coax her out myself, and I now felt like a fool, filled with the shame I feel after any social call where I've tried to ingratiate myself, to charm. Why had I told her about my trip to Paris with Mourad before I'd come to Egypt? Why, when she'd asked how long I would be staying, had I thought she needed to know I'd only be here three weeks because I was spending August in Cape Cod? If my husband had been with me, we would have shared a laugh at the clash of classes taking place in the al-Sadr living room. Many women passed through my mind: women with whom I'd had things in common only for our friendships to fall apart before their time. One reason for those failures, I thought to myself, was the mask with which the Egyptian bourgeoisie protects itself. A person might be anxious and fragile, open and intimate, but the instant they sense a threat, without even being conscious of making the decision, they will start to make a display of their class; they'll tell you about their Turkish grandmother, say, or their father's library of French literature. If Enayat had been anything like this, then she lived among us still. I wore the mask myself whenever I felt exposed or vulnerable in their presence. I had wanted to make Azima aware of who I was, of my circumstances: that I traveled the world, that I was an academic, that my time was precious.

Enayat (far left) with her family at al-Qanatir al-Khayriyyah

A breeze made me feel better. The thread of life down which I was feeling my way had had its kinks and knots smoothed out, leaving me with a picture-perfect image of the happy family: the cultured father who worked at Cairo University, a pasha's granddaughter for a mother, and three daughters, all of whom studied at the German School and married early. Enayat "just had bad luck." With the bourgeoisie as their custodians, facts became secrets, the name of her husband a personal matter, and as for the address where she lived and killed herself or the location of the tomb where her remains had been laid, well . . . "What do you want these addresses for? Are you writing about her, or about her apartment and her grave?"

No trace of Enayat's personal life had survived beyond those relics that are always kept by respectable families following the death of one of their respectable members: family portraits. The journals had been destroyed in 1963, the year of their author's death, with only a few pages allowed to survive and be published: "It was a private journal, and there's no need to go digging up old hurt. She used to fill lots of little black notebooks, like the one you're holding." Her letters? "We didn't think anyone would be interested." The unpublished stories? "I was always abroad with my husband. It was Aida who looked after her papers after my father passed. He died on January 30, 1971. I asked Aida's children, and they told me they'd got rid of all the old junk when they'd repainted the flat in Zamalek."

I remembered what I'd hoped for and laughed.

The next day, I traveled up to my father's house in Mansoura for Eid. I arrived after dark and had to grope around for the keys. I couldn't remember having ever used them before: my father or his wife were usually home. They must be at the prophet's tomb receiving blessings by now. I had flown in to Cairo the week before, and no sooner had I arrived at my apartment than my sister Sanaa had called to say that our parents were on their way from Mansoura to the airport, and that we should all go to see them off.

At the airport they told us they'd be staying in Saudi Arabia until it was time for hajj. My father had produced the house keys with a dramatic flourish: "Iman, Sanaa is spending Eid in the Fayoum with her husband's family, but our house must be open and you must be there to manage things. We've got everything set up: cakes and qurabiya, pastries, tirmis and carob juice—the lot. Everything you like is sitting in the freezer. Open the house up and invite your aunt and her children."

What to do, as they say. I had struggled fruitlessly for an excuse, while Sanaa stood next to my father, nodding along with his words and winking at me. So here I was: opening my father's house and hunting for the switches by the glow of my phone.

Being there alone, I felt strangely at peace. After I'd showered and had a cup of tea, I crossed the street to Mohammed Shams al-Din's store, and asked if he had any heavy-duty cardboard boxes. Mohammed had grown up next door to my grandfather and his elder sister had been in my class before dropping out of school in year four. "Don't worry about it. You go home now and the boxes will come to you."

So home I went, up to the shed on the flat roof to look for my things. There was nothing up there but washing lines. I called my father in Saudi Arabia. "What are you doing up there? We keep your stuff in the storeroom next to the house. You'll need the square key."

Mohammed made his delivery, and I spent the night sorting through my papers, throwing some away and packing others into pristine Ariel boxes. And when the Eid prayers began to drift over from Hagg Ragab's threshing floor, I locked up the house and went to sleep.

9.

No map of Dokki makes any mention of an Astra Square, nor Abdel Fattah al-Zeini Street for that matter. Was Nadia sure about the names?

"Enayat's home was my home. There was a creamery on the square called Astra Dairy. Just ask around. It was the best dairy in Egypt."

Astra might have been the best dairy in Egypt the last time Nadia went to Enayat's house, but that had been over fifty years ago.

I decided that I would embark on a series of free-ranging walks and see what I could turn up. My first little expedition ran from Mesaha Square to the residential blocks by Orman Garden. It had been more than twenty-five years since I had lived here as a student, but the streets still seemed familiar. I combed the pavements on the lookout for older doormen, whom I would first salute and then interrogate: "Astra Dairy? Abdel Fattah al-Zeini?" I'd get a story about the old name of the street I was standing in, say, or a mansion that had been demolished. There was the grand old family that had once lived here but had gone abroad, the shop that had been another shop in the old days, there was even one account of a tree that had been cut down to make room for a building, but not one of them remembered Astra.

The next day I set out again, this time from Vini Square. In Hindawi Street, Hagg Abdel Hamid called me over to come and sit with him on his bench. He'd been sixteen when he came up to Cairo from the village of Shaturma in Aswan to work in a mansion. Retired now, he was provided for by his grandson, who was doorman for one of the two apartment blocks erected on the site of the old mansion. He told me about the death of his only child, electrocuted while fixing the lights in the building's stairwell, then that his grandson was not only doorman of the building but one of the most influential rental agents in the neighborhood. "Astra Dairy?" he said. "That became Egypt Dairy long ago. Look for a square with an Egypt Dairy and you'll find what you're after."

The doormen are guardians of entire geographies. Incomers from tiny villages, they not only watch over their assigned building, cleaning its stairs and running errands for its residents, they also catalog every detail of the built environment through which they move. As though the cramped rooms they inhabit, usually at street level or below, are closed-circuit cameras recording everything that passes their lenses.

In 1956, Gamal Abdel Nasser called for "a cup of milk for every child," and set up the Egypt Dairy Company to make it possible. It began with a factory in Amiriyah, then expanded its reach, with factories in Mansoura, Alexandria, Tanta, Kom Ombo and Sakha.

By the time Abdel Nasser passed, Egypt Dairy owned a vast fleet of refrigerated trucks for distributing milk and yogurt nationwide and was the largest dairy company in the Middle East. Thanks to nationalization, the company was granted numerous outlets in Cairo and Alexandria by the government, and purchased additional properties for the same purpose.

Reading through this report on Egypt Dairy, I remembered hearing somewhere that, as a young man, the film director Atef al-Tayyeb had worked as a milkman for his father's little creamery; the creamery, it transpired, had been in Dokki, and had gone under in 1963.

I wanted to go back to thank Hagg Abdel Hamid. It was because of him that I'd thought to read this report at all. I would tell the old man how the company had begun to be broken up and privatized under the Mubarak regime, its factories sold off through secretive tenders, their employees released and their equipment either auctioned or put into storage and declared scrap, before being illicitly sold to private dairies. That, though Egypt Dairy had returned to the limelight in 2008 when the laid-off workers from the Amiriyah factory demanded it be reopened, a committee from the Ministry of Health had advised against reopening due to structural flaws in the building, and because tiles were falling off the walls and the taps were leaking. That the only Astra I could find was Astra Tourism in Mesaha Square, that the only dairy I'd heard of was Egypt Dairy in Dokki Street (courtesy of Hagg Abdel Hamid), yet neither of these had the slightest connection with a street called Abdel Fattah al-Zeini.

Three expeditions into Dokki had taught me that the neighborhood contained a limitless supply of squares. Every and any intersection seemed to bear the name, and anything on foot now seemed whimsical and doomed to failure.

I found a site on the internet belonging to something that called itself the Public Authority for Surveying. The site contained a brief history of the body since its foundation:

On February 9, 1879, Khedive Tawfiq formally inaugurated the Egyptian Land Survey Administration, falling under the control of the Ministry of Finance. On February 23, 1887, the Land Survey Administration was transferred to the Ministry of Public Works, and the administration's work continued until the cabinet meeting of June 16, 1898, which issued a decree establishing the General Surveying Agency, under control of the Ministry of Public Works, tasked with providing a detailed survey of agricultural land in Egypt using the most exact and scientific methods, in order to facilitate tax collection by the state. The agency remained a part of the Ministry of Public Works until 1905, when it was returned to the Ministry of Finance.

It went on to describe the agency pinballing between different ministries following the 1952 revolution. The word used for *Land Survey* at the start of the passage was *ta'ree'*. I'd never seen it before. It wasn't in the dictionary but, thinking it could be derived from *taqree'*, I did find the following based on the same verbal root: *'ard qara'* being *land in which nothing grows*, and *assaaha quri'at* meaning *the area is unpopulated*. So: one of those words invented and deployed in old texts, where it sits, moribund, until disinterred and reanimated in a modern context. Maybe it was first written down by the scribe of the land tax register following the Islamic conquests;

maybe it was a loan word, a reframed and distorted version of Turkish bureaucratic terminology that appeared under the Ottoman Empire. I said it out loud over and over in order to taste its peculiarity, and recalled that—somewhere in the nineteenth-century texts I'd assembled while researching Rashid Pasha—there had been some reference to a surveying administration in the reign of Khedive Ismail.

But before I could get back to my files, another thought struck me: that the information on the website was inaccurate in at least one respect, because Tawfiq Pasha had not been khedive on February 9, 1879, but rather the regent, and that he'd only succeeded his father, Ismail, in July. Returning to Ilyas al-Ayoubi's history, I saw that there was indeed an agency called the Land Survey Administration, but that it used the conventional term for survey, *mesaha*, and not *ta'ree'*. There was also something about the Mesaha School, which Ali Mubarak relocated along with a number of other schools from Abbasiya to the Palace of Amir Mustafa Fadel in Gamameez Lane in 1868.

Elsewhere, al-Ayoubi writes about the two commissioners, one French and one British, that objected to Sharif Pasha's government being composed entirely of Egyptians. That when the cabinet was formed on April 10, 1879, they both resigned, and were joined by Auckland Colvin, head of the cadastral survey.

The authority's main office was at No. 1, Abdel Salam Aref Street in Orman. I must have passed it hundreds of times between 1988 and 1991 without noticing it was there: it was on the route between my student accommodation in Mesaha Street and Cairo University.

Nor, I now realized, had I ever asked myself why the area where I lived was called Mesaha.

"I'd like to buy a map of the Dokki neighborhood as it was around 1960 or 1961, please. I need the names of streets and squares to be clearly marked as well."

"This is the registry office. Land valuations, property transfers, and major developments."

"I . . ."

"The land survey offices are on Haroun Street. It's very close, and you can buy your map of Dokki there before one."

It was twenty past eleven, the first working day after Eid al-Fitr. Instead of running to Haroun Street, perhaps encouraged by the evident sincerity of the young woman helping me, I assumed the demeanor of the upright citizen and produced my mobile phone. Scrolling through the gallery of images, I said that I would very much appreciate it if she could look at what the Public Authority for Surveying had up on its website, and confirm whether it was true. "You see," I said, "there are passages in Ilyas al-Ayoubi's history which suggest the Land Survey Authority was formed *before* Tawfiq Pasha became . . ." She was staring at me in frank astonishment. I must have sounded ridiculous, a little unhinged, even. Maybe she had never considered the possibility of a citizen coming in to correct the government.

"Like, are you a professor of history or something?"

"No, no."

Kindly now, she advised me to send all the information I had directly to the email listed on the authority's website.

I thanked her. Before I could reach the door she called out:

"Go via Mesaha Square. The security forces have closed Haroun Street from this end. You take a right and when you get to Haroun Street take another right and ask for Coiffeur Saeed: you want the building facing the hairdresser. When you get there, ask for Mohammed Mahmoud."

Five minutes later, I had Coiffeur Saeed to my right; to my left was a high wall with two large gates, both ornately worked in wrought iron and both padlocked shut. A cigarette kiosk stood between these gates, and then a little farther along was a tiny gate of sheet metal. The hole for the gate had been cut straight into the wall, as though chiseled out of a cliff. A tall person would have to stoop to get through, a wide one to wedge themselves in and squeeze through. In front of me, standing isolated in the middle of an open space, was one of those airport security scanners, watched over by an unmanned checkpoint. Beyond this was a neglected garden of huge trees, which shielded the main building from the street.

A few steps led up and into the entrance hall. The wall to the right was hung with maps, and to the left ran a long rectangular table loaded with cake and biscuits and teacups at which sat three women. I broke in on the gathering with a request for Mohammed Mahmoud. One of them gestured to a doorway across the hall: "There's no Mohammed Mahmoud here, but there is a Mahmoud Mohammed. He might do?" They laughed and I laughed with them, hopes buoyed by their good humor.

Mahmoud Mohammed was sitting alone, surrounded on all sides by heaped files, and fronted by the heavy frame of his spectacles. His thick head of hair aside, he was the very image of a government bureaucrat as portrayed in Egyptian cinema of the eighties. But he was extremely cooperative. "The map won't help you," he said. "You need to take this form"—he passed me a document entitled Name Changes—"and enter the street name you're looking for." I decided that I wanted both: form and map. On the form I wrote my name, ID number, address, and telephone number, and finally, the words *Abdel Fattah al-Zeini Street*. He gazed at my work with satisfaction. Now, he said, you go to the window, pay thirty-five pounds and seventy piastres, then leave the form with the Changes Department.

I went downstairs. There was a long, almost totally unlit corridor, its walls so thickly papered with documents and official announcements that office doorways were impossible to see until you were directly opposite them. The woman whom I'd first met grazing on Eid cake told me to come back tomorrow to collect "your name."

Then, curious: "What's it about? An inheritance thing, or a case against the Ministry of Endowments?"

"Oh no," I said, "nothing like that. I'm just researching family history."

This, I felt, wasn't so far from the truth.

I left the building in high spirits. If only I could wait here until it opened tomorrow. I offered my sincerest thanks to Mahmoud Mohammed, to the witty women, to the well-bred bureaucrats of yesteryear who'd dreamed up such wonders as *ta'ree'* and *mesaha* and the Name Changes form.

There was a café next to Coiffeur Saeed, and I went in and sat down. The window at the back of the café looked out over a court, surrounded on two sides by a hulking contemporary building, tempered-glass balconies overhanging the flight of steps that led up to its first-floor entrance. My eye drifted over a sign—*Studio Béla*—and I did a double-take.

The story goes that the original photography studio, six hundred square meters on Qasr al-Nil Street, had been founded in 1890 by a Hungarian called Béla; after passing through the hands of several European owners, the business ended up in the possession of an Egyptian at some point in the 1950s. This Egyptian had taken the founder's name as his own, and it had been Mohieddin Béla himself who had taken my wedding portraits, crouched behind the lens of his venerable Linhof. For years afterwards, one of the portraits of my husband and I had been on display in the studio's glass shopfront. On my last trip to Egypt I had taken a wedding photo and gone to see him, hoping to get a crack on the back of the frame repaired, but where the studio once stood on Qasr al-Nil Street there'd been a shoe shop. A newspaper seller outside the building had told me that Hagg Béla was long dead and that the building's owners had won a court case and managed to evict his son, Ashraf Béla, from the property. He didn't know where Ashraf had taken the business, but he had his number.

I'd saved the number on my phone, but never called.

Now, I drank down my tea and went over to the shop. It was closed for the day. There was a small, dusty window, in which sat one ancient camera and a pair of portraits: one of the actress Hind Rustom, the other of the preacher Sheikh Metawalli al-Shaarawi.

Down Haroun Street I went, a person with nothing to do until tomorrow afternoon, inspecting every tree, every building, every balcony. How many streets had I walked down in my life, as blind to my surroundings as someone with their eyes rolled inwards? And what about these signs by the doorbells! No. 5, *Graduates of the al-Nokrashy Pasha Model School*; No. 12, *The Bismillah Institute for Cultural Services and Development* and *The Rotary Club of Cairo, Wadi Digla Branch*; No. 12A, *The Business Council of Egypt and Sudan*; No. 13, *The Scientific Association for Economic Education*; No. 14, *Members Club for the Staff of Cairo University* and *The Egyptian Society for the Sciences & Halal Products*; No. 15, *The Haggan Institute for Teaching Critical Thought*.

Abdel Fattah al-Zeini Street became Sherbiny Street in 1963, when it was officially incorporated into the neighborhood of Dokki. If you walk down al-Tahrir Street into Dokki Square, coming from the Cairo Opera House, the next street to your right leading off the square is Mihallawi Street. Turn down Mihallawi and keep going, pushing your way through the pavement sellers who have spilled out from Soleiman Gowhar Market to occupy the surrounding streets, and after no more than four minutes you will reach the point where Sherbiny meets Mihallawi and Soleiman Gowhar. Sherbiny Street runs from Dokki Street down to this modest junction—the place Nadia knew as Astra Square—then continues on for another one hundred meters or so to terminate at the dead end of a narrow alley.

In January 1963 only a small number of families lived here. To the right of anyone entering from Dokki Street was the two-story villa and garden where Taha Fawzi lived alone. Next door to the villa was the Magediya, a private Arabic-language school which ran through kindergarten, primary, and secondary, and had been founded in 1947 by Ziyad Ghannam al-Magedy. It was closed down by order of the Labor Court in 1963 for failing to pay teachers' salaries. Across the road from the villa and the school was a plot of land leased by the school as a playground. When the school went under, all three properties—school, villa, and playground—were purchased by an importer of Chinese goods from Damietta called al-Halwani, who built two large apartment blocks on either side of the street. His son still owns them and lives in one of them. Many of the street's old villas have been replaced by these swarming close-packed buildings, but the villa at No. 9 is still there. Post-nationalization, it was converted into a residence for Sudanese military officers training in Egypt, then in the 1980s it became a hostel for Palestinian students. It is now something called the Arab and African Women's Development Foundation.

Abbas Hilmi al-Zayyat built his home in 1957, a three-story building at No. 16. He occupied the ground floor and Enayat lived on the second. After his death in 1971 the house was sold, four more floors were added, and a section of the ground floor was converted into a commercial premise: al-Sharif al-Nawwal Paints. The shop is still there. A municipal map from the period shows that across the street from al-Zayyat's house stood a villa, the Mihallawi Villa, named after one of the senior sheikhs of al-Azhar in the 1930s, Sheikh al-Mihallawi, but on his death his son Saad al-Mihallawi leveled the villa and threw up an apartment block in its place. The

Astra Dairy hung on until 1965, on the corner where Abdel Fattah al-Zeini meets Soleiman Gowhar. Soleiman Gowhar Street itself had yet to become an open-air market. Today, the dairy is just another apartment block.

Behind Astra Dairy was an open plot planted with trees, property of the Maqar family. The plot was subsequently divided into quarters, three of which were subsequently developed, leaving a single subplot which is now a fenced-off patch of waste ground filled with trash, the word *Bibo* (a football player's nickname) daubed on its outer wall.

Facing this former grove there were once four villas. Villa Maqar, which looked out on the intersection, is now an apartment block undergoing renovations. The other three villas have been spared, though each is capped by either two or three additional floors.

Later, I will enter one of these villas, to meet Madame al-Nahhas, a friend of Enayat's and one of the oldest and longest-standing residents on the street. She will tell me that the older people in the area know her as Madame al-Nahhas, not because it was her name, but because the former prime minister, al-Nahhas Pasha, had been a close friend of her father, himself a senior figure in the Wafd Party back in the day. She will tell me that her husband had been a Wafd man, too, and had been raised on the teachings of al-Nahhas Pasha, who had been a frequent visitor to his home, as he had been to hers. But she was not a member of the family.

On another of my many subsequent trips, I will sit with Ghannam, son of the Magediya School's founder, outside the al-Sharif al-Nawwal Paints store, retracing the map of the street as it had been and those who had lived there. He will tell me that the school killed his father, and will complain bitterly about the Labor Court's ruling. The school had gone bankrupt, he will say, because his father took in the children of poor families and refused to charge them. He will tell me, too, about the many important people who passed through its doors: the actor Saeed Saleh, Hassan al-Abdeen, who went on to become an ambassador, and the famous engineer whose name he couldn't remember, but who'd been head of the surveying authority in Dokki. When he said *surveying authority* I lifted my gaze to Enayat's second-floor balcony and imagined that she was still up there, that she'd been there since January 3, 1963, standing motionless behind the wire screen which stretched across the windows.

10.

No sooner had Reda opened the door than I was greeted
effusively by four tiny pugs, snouts like rucked-up sleeves
around their flattened noses. I sat down to wait in the living
room while the pugs snuffled round me, making friends.
What was the proper word for pugs in Arabic, again? We
were calling them *buhgz* but that couldn't be right. I was
surrounded by pictures of Nadia, stills from her films, portraits taken at different times of her life, but two photographs
were larger than the rest. In one, she sits smiling on the sofa,
while Yasser Arafat stands behind her, his keffiyeh the match
of the one she wears draped across her shoulders. She is also
with Arafat in the second. He is dressed in military fatigues
and she stands alongside him; they are surrounded by men.
Both must date from her famous visit to meet the Palestinian
resistance fighters during the Israeli siege of Beirut in 1982.

The dogs all looked identical, impossible to tell apart on
casual acquaintance. Then it came to me: *salsaal*! That was
the word for a pug. When Reda came in to offer me a cup
of water, I apologized. Sorry for bothering you with all those

calls this past fortnight. She gave a wary smile. Madame would be here shortly. Reda didn't talk to guests.

Nadia made an entrance in Indian attire: white billowing trousers and a blouse of embroidered light white fabric, a length of which was also wrapped around her head. Here, on home ground, she seemed genial and at ease. I, by contrast, was making an effort. I'd had my hair done at Halim's salon in Mohandiseen, whose walls are covered in portraits of Halim with famous actresses, then prayed the humidity wouldn't ruin everything before she got to see it. I wore a short, sleeveless, copper-colored dress and matching sandals, and because I'd never worn them together I was feeling nervous as a peasant on her first trip to the city. She greeted me, set a large bag full of photographs and papers on the table, then embraced me and sat.

I felt that shiver run through me, the way you do when meeting someone you feel you've known your whole life, though in fact you're only in their presence for the first time, only now sharing their time and space. The sensation is the physical manifestation of an acute and entirely one-sided awareness, a desire to balance the equation, to not be a fool, to not squander your energy in astonishment.

For the first time in our acquaintance, Nadia asked me about myself, and when she heard I was from Mansoura, she told me the story of how, in 1986, she had gone to see the writer Fouad Higazi there and recorded his account of being captured as a prisoner of war by the Israelis in 1967. I didn't tell her that Fouad had been my mentor during that period, and that I, too, had visited him at his apartment in Sheikh Hassanein. She had filmed interviews with a large number of prisoners of war for a documentary project, but had no idea where the tapes were now.

What was this "Townhouse Gallery" I'd gone to yesterday night, she wanted to know? Had I talked about Enayat? Her memory was incredible. The morning before I'd called her up to say that time was running out and that I only had a few days left in Cairo, and she had invited me over that evening. I'd apologized profusely and said that I had to give a talk, and she had seemed both displeased and dismissive of my excuse.

Well, no, I said, not about Enayat. It was an open discussion about my research and reading and my writing in general. It was the first time she had heard that I was a writer, too. And something happened which I hadn't anticipated: this simple piece of information cast a spell over the entire evening. "Why didn't you say so!" she said. "I thought you were an academic doing a paper on Enayat or something." My haircut and outfit had been pointless, then; all she'd needed to feel comfortable with me was the knowledge that I was a writer, that we were both "artists."

I told her I was married and had two sons and she asked how I managed to balance writing with the children. My husband, I said. He does his share and more. I told her that one of the boys was currently in Boston, taking a series of difficult exams to get into a private school there. I wasn't there with him, of course, and I didn't feel happy about having him leave home at just fifteen. She said that when her son Ahmed was still young, she'd sent him to study in America in the care of her Aunt Nana, and that she'd flown over to see him when she could, while he would visit her in the summer. She said that a mother who was an artist must harden her heart. Which is how motherhood brought us to Enayat:

"In our generation, mine and Enayat's, the social change was enormous. Working in cinema wasn't frowned on anymore; a woman could be a writer and a painter. Abdel Nasser wanted to make the arts a first line of defense, a front. There was a revival of music and dance and women were welcomed in. There was an equality there. Enayat and I, we were pioneers. We were believers; we truly believed in Abdel Nasser. But Enayat didn't know how to harden her heart. Her son and her writing were the air she breathed. The last time I saw her was that Thursday morning: January 3, 1963. I was getting myself together to go up to Alexandria for my birthday, and she was supposed to be coming with me. She was already heartbroken because the boy was going to go to his father. The lawyers had used her prescription for depression medication as evidence against her in the custody battle. And then, when she got home from court, she found that al-Qawmiyya had called and told her mother that the novel wasn't fit to publish."

"You mean she never phoned you in Alexandria, the way it's written up in your interview with Foumil Labib?"

"No. I got back to Cairo about five in the morning on January 4. I'd meant to call her as soon as I got in, but I was distracted, and then that evening they were all calling me up and saying, Send Enayat back home, would you? Which is when I said she'd never come. They found her the morning of January 5, like I told you before."

There was something strange about this account of the al-Qawmiyya incident, I said. I'd read an article by the critic Hilmi Sallaam in which he'd written: *Nadia, when she talked about Enayat, never tired of saying that in her friend she had found the other half of her existence. And that despite all the many events and excitements of Nadia Lutfi's life, she would always return, compelled, to Enayat al-Zayyat, who ended her life as though it was a Greek tragedy. One simple error, and a phone call, then . . . then Enayat committed suicide. Maybe it had been fate on the other end of the line . . .*

"What error?" I asked.

"OK, I didn't want to talk about this before because it really is a Greek tragedy. There'd been some idea that Azima could translate literary texts from German to Arabic. So Azima had sent off a proposal and a sample for the publisher to look at, but it turned out that the only German books they were interested in were about Ancient Egypt and Islamic history. Azima had also left her husband, and was living on the first floor of her parents' building in Dokki. She had a divorce going through the courts and a custody battle, the same as Enayat. Poor Uncle Abbas,

Enayat (left) and Nadia Lutfi

God have mercy on him, he suffered a lot. Anyway, on January 3, al-Qawmiyya calls to say the book's not fit to publish. Then two or three days later they call again and the mother takes it, and they say, Sorry, we weren't referring to Enayat's novel. We meant Azima's translations."

"Fuck," I said, in English. I'm sure Nadia heard.

There was a minute's silence while I tried to collect myself. I had visited Azima, I told her, just before Eid. I hadn't known that she'd been living in the building as well, nor that she'd been interested in translation. I hadn't known about al-Qawmiyya's error. But then that was odd, too. If the novel had been fit to publish after all, why had it taken another four years, till March 1967, for it to be released?

Eagerly, Nadia asked for Azima's phone number, then told Reda to place the call for her. I sat there, listening to the conversation between two women who hadn't met for decades.

Nadia put the phone down and resumed where she'd left off:

"I don't know what to say. The first time they called they said Enayat's novel had been rejected, and by the time they corrected their mistake, she'd killed herself."

Her voice grew strangled.

I didn't know what to say.

My guess was that al-Qawmiyya had been upset by the suggestion that a writer had killed herself because they had rejected her book. Maybe, too, a few of the arts journalists had caught wind of the story after Nadia Lutfi suffered a nervous breakdown. Al-Qawmiyya's second call to the family could have been a way of shifting responsibility. Smoke and mirrors.

Nadia opened the bag and pulled out a stack of photographs showing her and Enayat together: swimming at Ras al-Barr and Alexandria, racing their bicycles, strolling through the Merryland Gardens. I asked about their clothes. Why did they seem to be wearing matching outfits in so many of the pictures? She said that they used to shop for fabric together, pick an outfit from the magazines or films, then take the fabric to a certain Madame Aflatoun to make up into dresses. Even swimsuits.

"Like that famous striped bikini Marilyn Monroe wore. The dancer Samia Gamal did a shoot in one just like it. We took the photo and had a pair made for ourselves."

Surely this must have stopped when Nadia became involved in films, I told myself. The pictures were prompting Nadia to tell me all the things I'd wanted to hear from her, like the times Enayat came to visit her on the sets of *My Only Love* and *Come Back, Mother*. She showed me an autographed photograph from 1950, on the back of which Enayat had written, *You are my sister.* Then she showed me photographs of the actresses she had been crazy about before she got into acting herself. One was of Faten Hamama. It had been a gift from Enayat, she told me, and she had taken it from *al-Kawakib* magazine, the May 1954 issue.

She gave me just seven pages from Enayat's journal. I was just fighting the urge to read them on the spot, when Nadia herself began to read from one of them. But then she changed her mind and handed it over:

Woman at the window, beautiful and sad, it is to your vague, distracted gaze, to the glum sickles beneath your lovely eyes, to your eyes full of misery, pain, and grief, that I write this poem. Between kitchen-cleaning and tile-scrubbing, dishes and nappies, between cooking the supper and ironing your husband's shirt, you are a woman adrift: all at sea and a brute for a husband, with his noontime demands, his long snoring sleeps, and not one tender word or caress. Poor girl, slaving for a husband, your eyes tell it all. At the end of the day you sit by the window, staring with clouded eyes into the distance, dreaming the past, dreaming the dreams of virginal girls, of words of love, so beautiful and far away—and then you rise and in the cracked mirror contemplate what traces remain of your beauty—no use—no traces remain—all lost to exhaustion, to unflagging insomnia, to a husband's cruelty, to He Who Must Be Obeyed. I can see it in your

*Nadia and Enayat (right)
at Ras al-Barr*

burning distracted gaze, looking out past the people and objects that surround you to the magical world of your own imagining, where no one can persecute you, no one enslave you, no one crowd your world with their power, their Man-the-Leader and Woman-the-Follower.

Nadia said that Enayat wrote this entry while she was still living with her husband, and that during this period she used to entrust her private papers to Nadia's safekeeping.

Buoyed, I asked about the box she'd mentioned,

the one next to the bed in the guest room. She called Reda in and instructed her to fetch it. Reda disappeared and the conversation shifted towards the Muslim Brotherhood and President al-Sisi. I barely got a word in.

She began to tell me how she got her start in cinema, about the cocktail party at her mother-in-law's house in Heliopolis: "John Khoury and his wife Marcelle were there. Khoury said he wanted to set up a new cinema production company and my mother-in-law was keen to become a partner. Marcelle turned to her husband and said, 'What about Paula for your next film, John?' Now the producer Ramses Naguib was also at the party, and when he heard this he said, 'Wonderful idea!' and promised me a part in his next film."

Nadia went to the bathroom. Reda had still not reappeared.

I thought about coincidence, how it had played a genuinely significant role at the time. The film stars of this generation had seen their destinies switch between obscurity and fame with astonishing ease. As though fate was a wanton boy, toying with this generation in transition, shuttling them back and forth between cocktail parties and social change and al-Qawmiyya and Abdel Nasser's "cultural battlefront."

Nadia said, "Ramses Naguib had a board which examined me and tested my acting, and I passed. On the board was Galil al-Bandari, Abdel Nour Khalil, Foumil Labib, Ihsan Abdel Quddous and Youssef al-Sebaie. Ramses was a great producer. He brought fine art into set design and introduced me to the illustrator Bahgat Osman, to Aboul Ainein and Shadi Abdel Salam, who did the decor for this apartment by the way."

"What, Shadi Abdel Salam the director?" I said. "Our Shadi Abdel Salam?"

"No," she said, "mine," and we laughed.

"Some of the first people I got to know after I began in cinema were Ahmed Ragab, Anis Mansour and Mustafa Mahmoud. I was at the Equestrian Club with Wigdan al-Barbary. She was the wife of Dr. al-Barbary and those three were friends of his. I brought them samples of Enayat's writing and they liked it. In 1959, or maybe 1960, Mustafa Mahmoud published some short stories of hers in *Sabah al-Kheir*. They were almost like poems. He ran them under a pen name."

Why a pen name, I wanted to know, and what was it?

"I don't remember. Enayat was in the middle of her ordeal with the divorce. The case was still ongoing and she asked that her name not appear."

And had Anis Mansour published any stories of hers as well?

"No," she said.

"Youssef al-Sebaie used to visit the set while we were filming *Saladin*. We were rehearsing and so on from 1959. Filming stopped for a while, then it started up again. Now of course Shadi Abdel Salam was there, as well as the composer Mohammed Sultan who, by the way, owned the building next door to my father's in Alexandria—his father used to run a riding school where I'd go to take lessons. Anyway, the point is that Enayat and I went to meet Youssef al-Sebaie at the writers' club, one night in the summer of 1960. The club was right round the corner in Garden City. We gave him the manuscript of the novel, the one written in pencil, for him to read and decide whether it was worth publishing or not."

So Enayat had finished the novel in 1960?

"Yes. I'm sure of the date because she wasn't divorced yet."

Had Enayat taken her novel to Anis Mansour, I asked? What about the suggestions he made, which she rejected?

"She never went to his office."

And Nadia had one final surprise to unveil. She said that she felt guilty, because at the time she hadn't understood how the literary world worked. She had imagined that these writers would see how talented Enayat was and would publish her. She began to take me through photographs of her posing with the men she considered true writers. All had been taken after Enayat's death, after she'd read more and learned more: Youssef Idris, Louis Awad, Ahmed Baha Eddin, Lotfi al-Khouli, and other luminaries. She gave me some to keep. For a reason I didn't fully understand at the time, this left me feeling flustered. In the years that followed, this agitation would return every time Nadia told me something she had never spoken of to the press. Maybe it was nothing more than the tension between my desire to know everything Nadia had to tell me and my fear of the responsibility this would bring: that I would be compelled to write about it.

As we waited for Reda to return with the box, Nadia asked me when she could read what I'd written about Enayat. I assured her that I'd have a draft to send her by next December. I believed it at the time, but my miscalculation was to generate a degree of strain in our relationship. Whenever she subsequently returned to this question, I would do my best to avoid giving her an answer.

What happened was that, after returning home from Egypt in 2015, I went back to writing about motherhood. For about a year and a half afterwards, I was entirely occupied by this project, my teaching, and travel. I was traveling once a month on average, either to Utah to visit my son Youssef at his boarding school, or to Boston where my other boy Mourad was attending high school, or to attend readings I'd agreed to give and which it was impossible to back out of. Enayat receded ever further into the background. Whenever she crossed my mind, I would go back to the chapter I was working on and change a word here or there, or make a call to Nadia or Azima in Cairo. Just a call, to ask them how they were.

Nadia called out to Reda again to bring the box. There was no answer. I offered to go and see where she was. Right beside the apartment's front door was another, smaller door. I opened it: a passageway led to a kitchen. I called her name in the same tone Nadia had used. I could hear Reda talking on the phone, finishing a call. I heard, or thought I heard, her say, "Don't worry. I'll tell them I couldn't find it. I already said I was going to ask you."

"What box?" Reda said when she'd rejoined us in the room, "I can't find anything . . ." Then she withdrew again, pursued by Nadia's shrieked command to look again. It was clear to me that scenes of this nature were not infrequent. Reda must have been phoning Nadia's son, I thought. She wasn't just "the help" or a secretary, but a member of the family. She'd come north as a young woman, to keep Nadia company and take care of her, and quite possibly she kept an eye on her on Ahmed Adel al-Beshari's behalf, protecting her from conmen and roving journalists. And fair enough. If Nadia was my mother, living alone in a country like Egypt, I would no doubt do the same.

I realized that I would never get to see the box beside the bed in the guest room unless I was prepared to commit a crime: abduct Reda and spirit her out of the apartment. Then a thought: maybe I no longer needed these boxes and files to get to know Enayat.

II.

For thirty years, no conversation about the Egyptian actress Faten Hamama, or the journalist Hosn Shah, or the personal status laws, or the Arab Woman, or the power of cinema to bring about social change, could omit a reference to the 1975 film *I Want a Solution*. And this reference would almost always be followed by a piece of conventional wisdom: that President Anwar Sadat, prompted by the film and pressured by his wife, Jehan, granted Egyptian women the right to initiate divorce as well as a degree of protection from a cruel law which compelled them to return to the prisons of their marital homes. The discussion usually concludes with a word of praise: for Egyptian cinema, perhaps, or Faten Hamama, or Hosn Shah, or feminism—even for Sadat.

Hosn Shah wrote the screenplay for *I Want a Solution*. In an interview with Esam al-Sayyid for the *al-Hayat* newspaper, she said:

I have tried to tell a truth, something to benefit the society in which I live. My modest collection of films has had some impact.

Following the release of I Want a Solution, *the Egyptian govern-ment began considering changes to the personal status laws. It was the first dramatic work to openly discuss the idea of* khula—*or divorce initiated by women—a legal concept that had been kept in the dark for fourteen centuries, even though it is mentioned in the Quran. I drew attention to it. The law saved many women, among them the woman on whom I based the main character in my film. She spent twelve years of her life going through the courts and the story of the film is based on her experience. For me, it's enough to know that I was the reason for the personal status laws being changed.*

In several interviews, Hosn Shah states that her trans-formation from journalist to screenwriter was due to her former school friend, Faten Hamama, and that it was Faten Hamama who proposed they join forces and pitch a film about the personal status laws that would address the issue of delayed divorces and the infamous "obedience ruling," which compelled women to remain married against their will. A screenplay was written, only to be turned down by a number of producers on the grounds of its realism. Finally it was made: produced by Salah Zulfikar, directed by Saeed Marzouk, and released in 1975.

The Egyptian law to which Hosn Shah refers, the specific law which her film played a part in changing, was popu-larly known as the "house of obedience" law. This law gave husbands the right to refuse a request for divorce if they did not personally accept that there were sufficient grounds for complaint, obliging couples to turn to mediators in order to effect reconciliation. This would extend the period of litigation, particularly as husbands would often appeal the mediators' rulings if they proved unfavorable. And if the wife's grounds for divorce were not proven or accepted, then the husband had the right to demand she reside in a "house of obedience": a residence which the husband provides for her and which meets the legally prescribed conditions for a marital dwelling. That is to say: a home which is independent and secure, which allows the husband unfettered access, and which is appropriate to his wife's social standing.

At the time Enayat asked for her divorce, this law was the subject of fierce debate. Progressives argued that it had no foundation in Islamic law or fiqh, that the law was Ottoman or even Roman, or that the French had imported it during their Egyptian campaign. Some claimed that it hadn't existed at all prior to 1929. Its defenders maintained that it was irreproachably Islamic and that its existence provided a vital safeguard to social cohesion and the institution of the family.

Debates aside, there is no way of understanding what Enayat went through in the final years of her life without accepting this law as part of her story. It was not just a law, in other words, but one of the millstones which were slowly grinding her down and readying her for her end.

Issue 27 of the official gazette of Egypt, *Egyptian Affairs*, published on March 25, 1929—seven years less two days before Enayat was born—carries the text of Law 25 of that year, which gives guidance for rulings in personal status cases, such as divorce, maintenance payments, post-divorce marriages, custody, and establishing paternity. *By order of His Highness,*

King Fouad I, it concludes, *and his minister of justice, Ahmed Mohammed Khashaba, and Prime Minister Mohammed Mahmoud, this law is hereby enforced as a law of the land.*

Under the heading *Estrangement between the spouses and divorce on grounds of harm* the law contains the following articles:

6. *If the wife alleges harm towards her on the part of the husband which renders it impossible for her to remain among her family, she may ask the judge for a separation. At this point the judge may grant her a divorce if harm can be established and no reconciliation is possible. If the request is refused and her complaint repeated but no harm proven, then the judge must send for two mediators.*

7. *The two mediators must be men with a reputation for fairness and good sense. If possible, they must be related to the spouses; if this is not possible then they should be individuals with good knowledge of the parties' circumstances and the ability to mediate successfully between them.*

8. *The mediators must acquaint themselves with the grounds for the estrangement and do everything in their power to effect a reconciliation, in whatever way they see fit.*

9. *If the mediators are unable to effect a reconciliation, and the mistreatment is clearly from the side of the husband, or from both spouses, or if it is unclear who is at fault, then they may decide together to recommend a divorce.*

10. *If the two mediators are in disagreement, the judge may order them to reexamine the case. If the disagreement persists then he may appoint others in their place.*

11. *The mediators must present their recommendations to the judge and the judge must make the final ruling.*

As if to emphasise the importance of the mediators mentioned in the articles above, the text adds:

As the wife might demand maintenance from the husband for no other purpose than to exact revenge by extracting his money, and the husband might demand the imposition of the obedience law for no other reason than to strike down her maintenance claim and keep her under his control, subject to tyranny and abuse at his whim (not to mention the difficulties the above may cause in enforcing a ruling of obedience, or of maintenance payment on pain of imprisonment, and the criminal acts and damage that might result from continued estrangement), and having seen clear evidence of these negative consequences in legal complaints presented to it, the ministry prefers to continue following Imam Malik's rulings on estrangement between married couples, with the exception of those instances when the mediators take the view that the wife is solely at fault, since there is no justification for giving troublesome wives the incentive to air marital discord without good cause.

By the time *I Want a Solution* came out in 1975, Hosn Shah had already been campaigning against Law 25 for over a decade, describing it as the source of the injustices faced by Egyptian women in the personal status courts. Because wives were required to prove that their husbands had harmed them, they were drawn into the labyrinth of debating what constitutes evidence, coupled with the endless appeals of their husbands' lawyers, and should the court rule against the divorce on the grounds that harm was not proved, the husband had the right to demand they take up residence in a house of obedience. The law was enforced: wives who did not obey could be sent to prison like common criminals.

In 1967, Hosn Shah wrote a series of appeals in the pages of the *Akher Saa'a* magazine, addressed to one of the principal drafters of Egypt's civil code, Sheikh Farag al-Sanhouri, and then Minister of Justice, Esam Eddine Hasouna, both of whom were openly opposed to the abolition or amendment of the article dealing with obedience. She gave a number of accounts of Egyptian women whose lives she compared to the legally contested status of religious endowments in Egypt: left in limbo by the courts, neither married nor divorced.

One of the women Hosn Shah wrote about was Enayat's younger sister, Azima al-Zayyat. From September 1962, up until May 17, 1967 (the date Shah's article was published), Azima had been shuttling between the courts in pursuit of a divorce from her husband Mohammed Abdel Moneim al-Inbabi, a senior manager at the Iron and Steel Company.

Hosn Shah gave Azima's story a title: "Enayat al-Zayyat's Tragedy Replayed." It was effective, like all her titles, because although she was dealing only with Azima's case, she was able to link it to her dead sister's suffering at the hands of the same brutal law. It also tapped into the exposure that Enayat's name was getting with the publication of her novel only two months before. Shah wrote:

But who is Azima al-Zayyat? A quite ordinary citizen. Her father is among the very finest of men, one who has overseen the graduation of generation after generation of his students; he's an intellectual, and a provost at the university where he works. A man lucky enough to have three daughters: Enayat al-Zayyat, Azima al-Zayyat, and a third. Three daughters, all exceptional, all studying at the German School and graduating at the age of eighteen . . . only to marry, one after the other!

Then came the tragedy.

The tragedy of Enayat, which ended in suicide and the publication of a single novel, Love and Silence, *which the great critics all concur is a work of immense talent by a deeply sensitive woman. A woman who was yet to reach her twenty-fifth year on the day she killed herself.*

But why did Enayat al-Zayyat, this talented artist described by all who knew her as elegance and delicacy personified, commit suicide?

The critics and the writers say she ended her life because her novel was rejected, but—now I know Enayat's true story—I say different. I say that Enayat committed suicide because of cruelty. That a happy woman cannot kill herself over a book. That Enayat's disastrous married life had caused her such psychological and physical pain that her exhausted nerves betrayed her and led her to choose death over life.

And just like that, we lost a feminist genius who flared bright then faded all too soon into darkness.

The article made me think again about the father, Abbas al-Zayyat. I tried to picture him in 1962, bringing a divorce case on behalf of his youngest daughter, Azima, who had come back to live with him aged twenty-three and carrying a nursing infant, exactly as her older sister Enayat had done two years before.

Abbas al–Zayyat Effendi was born in Mansoura to a cultured landowning family and graduated from King Fouad I University in 1928. He was a friend to the romantic poets of the Apollo group in the 1940s and subscribed to the *al-Risala* magazine until it closed down in 1952; a man who sent his daughters to the German School and took them to the cinema (Paula with them) to watch new releases starring Faten Hamama or Audrey Hepburn; a father who found himself pitted against two successful and influential figures in the post-revolutionary Egyptian state, the first an air force officer from an important and well-regarded family, and the second a self-made man from the provinces who had taken advantage of the new political dispensation to elevate himself to senior management at the state-run Iron and Steel Company.

12.

On Wednesday, September 14, 1959, at the personal status court in Giza, citizen Enayat al-Zayyat brought Case 101 against Kamal Eddin Shaheen, requesting a divorce on the grounds of harm.

In her submission, the plaintiff states:

She married him on Thursday, November 8, 1956, and their marriage was consummated at his above-mentioned residence in Heliopolis. They were blessed with an only son, Abbas, whom she raised and cared for herself. On April 7, 1959, during the holy month of Ramadan, she left the marital home after their lives together had become a series of tragedies and degrading attacks by him against her as a woman, wife, and mother. She is requesting a divorce on the grounds of the harm done to her and the impossibility of resuming their former intimacy.

This first lawsuit contains no details concerning these *degrading attacks*, but this would change after the court rejected her case for failing to prove harm and she was forced to appeal.

I pictured Abbas al-Zayyat, sitting in the living room of his apartment with Nagi Khalil, a friend of the family who had also served as the family's lawyer ever since he had brought a case on Fahima Ali Abbas's behalf, asserting her right to the endowments of her grandfather, Ahmed Pasha Rashid. I pictured Enayat entering, sitting, and beginning to read through the text of the complaint. Maybe she was biting her lip, the way she did when something worried her. I pictured her asking Khalil to remove the description of her husband's assaults—they are humiliating—and suggesting instead: *their lives together had become a series of tragedies.*

This sentence is Enayat's, beyond a doubt. She could be so naïve in her writing: she believed that words had real weight in the world; that a word like *tragedies* might soften the heart of a judge, a husband even.

And she waited for the divorce to be granted, convincing herself that the law sought justice, that it would deliver her from the *tragedies* she was reluctant to describe even in the pages of her journal, as though the humiliations of her reality had to be softened by imagery, as though language could force a space between pain and the one who felt it.

She was naïve, then, still driven by hope. In her journals she would refer to herself in the third person:

She entered a marriage without love, without mutual under-standing, without compatibility. The possibility of such things had never occurred to her. Her only thought was to escape the discipline and constraints of school.

So the paradise of infancy closed its gates and the doors of a premature young adulthood swung open. Young adulthood? Just adulthood. And she chose wrong. She went through the wrong door, the one that opened onto a desert, onto wastelands devoid even of mirages, and she looked back to find that the door had vanished, and now there was no way home that she could see. Bewildered, she wept. Wretched and lost, she wept. And then she took heart and resigned herself. Resigned herself, and in doing so discovered an extraordinary capacity to endure. She saw herself as a camel, ruminating on all the happy moments of the past, chewing them over slowly, slowly in the midst of that brutal desert. And then? Then the provisions ran out, the past was finished, and the camel needed something new to chew on. But there was nothing to be had except despair, yellow as the sands, and her body wasted away and her soul thinned and she began to call for deliverance, began to scream for help. Suddenly she saw that her home was built on shifting sands and the harder she worked to save it the deeper and deeper it sank, and she pleaded for salvation, for help from God, from Fate, from everything. Caught up in her wild inquiry, she had forgotten that no one was coming to save her because she was the only one who could do it. The first impulse must be hers. Then she saw the key, the key of deliverance that hung at her neck and in her soul, in the spirit within her, and so she rose to her feet and, opening the door, she stood on the threshold and filled her lungs with life, with the rich fragrance of youth, the scent of spring and freedom. There on the threshold she cast off her old, cracked hide, gashed and knotted, saturated with fear, and took her first steps in new skin, free and uninhibited. She was brave, she was steadfast, she relied on herself.

When Enayat left her marital home and took her son with her, she returned, not to the apartment in Mounira where she'd been born and raised, but to her father's building in Dokki. And no sooner through the door than she asked for the empty apartment on the second floor: she wanted to be alone to finish her book. Abbas persuaded his wife Fahima to let their daughter be; told her that, after all, she was just upstairs. And then, because Enayat had only ever studied Arabic as a secondary language like French or English, she asked her father if he would teach her formal grammar. She began to read more Arabic.

The journal excerpt above must have been written during this period. The sensation that she describes as *freedom* was what she felt every evening after supper as she mounted the stairs to her apartment, to write alone.

At the time, it seems that the personal status courts liked to hand down their rulings quickly. Enayat's request for a divorce was turned down in November 1959, she appealed against this decision in January 1960, and by late May of that year, immediately before the Eid al-Adha holidays, her appeal was rejected, too.

According to the case file, the divorce was rejected because Enayat brought two women as separate witnesses to her allegations of her husband's humiliation of her: one a personal friend, the other her maid. Technically, the women's evidence was only valid if they testified together, for as the Quran has it:

Then summon two witnesses from among your men, and if two men are not to be found, then let it be one man and two women that satisfy you, so that if one errs in testimony, the other may remind her.

So, their separate testimony was an error in the eyes of the law, because the law required two women to testify together and concerning the same incident. Then, the file tells us, *the testimony of the male witness, her father, was dismissed because he had seen her crying but had not witnessed the incident that had made her cry, and furthermore he was her father.*

Maybe Enayat had to ask about words in the ruling she didn't understand then translate them to German in her head. Legal Arabic wasn't like the Arabic in which she wrote her novel. Nagi Khalil must have wanted to comfort her. He himself was deeply unhappy with the personal status laws. During the appeal process he expressed his position in court, a progressive lawyer taking a view of the law:

We were taught that a person has both rights and obligations before the law. That they are an independent and responsible individual and may be punished accordingly. In the Egyptian personal status laws, however, the woman is not a person, she is the property of her husband; she has been bought.

Waiting for a ruling on her appeal against the rejected appeal, Enayat copied out the manuscript of her novel in pencil, a copy she intended to give to Anis Mansour when he returned from his travels. This would never happen. One Wednesday after work, she climbed up to the ninth floor of 9 Bustan Street where Paula had recently rented an apartment, and the pair of them went out together, as they used to do before cinema had claimed all of Paula's time.

At the Writers' Association in Garden City, they met Youssef al-Sebaie. They sat down together and, as the women sipped lemon juice, Paula introduced Enayat:

"This is the friend I was telling you about. She's the one who introduced me to your work. She lent me *I Am Leaving* when we were at school and we watched *Give Back My Heart* and *Love Street* and *Among the Ruins* together. She's written a novel that's going to stun everyone."

Wordlessly, Enayat handed over the novel. Al-Sebaie and Paula began to talk animatedly of the producer Ramses Naguib and the film she'd just finished shooting with the director Kamal al-Sheikh. On the steps outside the club a young man working for *al-Kawakib* magazine approached Paula, greeted her fervently and declared, "Your role as the journalist in *Sultan* was a triumph both for the new woman and for politically conscious journalism and I must congratulate you!"

Paula took a step back, hand held out to shake his, and said with a star's wary reserve, "Well . . . thank you very much."

Later they would laugh at the incident. Paula would play the part of the eager young journalist and Enayat that of the actress, hopping backwards, left hand sweeping her skirt's hem aside, her right held out to be kissed.

During this period, as Enayat waited for the divorce to be granted, her journal entries were free of that former desperation. As though she had escaped her cage, and felt that no power on earth could put her back behind its bars. Now, suddenly, she was looking steadily and confidently at herself and towards her future:

Nothing can frighten me now. Death comes for those who tremble, for cowards, but I know why I'm here. I evolve because I choose to, because I choose to exist, and for the better. I have emerged out of who I was, stepping out of the frivolity of my daily life into something greater, something more profound. There's an understanding of what it means to exist, now, and a joy to be part of it, this existence, so broad and deep and full of secrets. Then there's the pleasure of discovering these secrets for myself: distant countries, enchanting music, thousands of books. So many things lie ahead. I love my existence. I hold tight to it, and to my youth and beauty, too, and to my undoubted desire to live, and live deeply.

Enayat had achieved something she had dreamed of since leaving her husband: she had saved enough from her salary to buy a typewriter.

Goldenstein & Sons ran an advertisement offering discounts on a range of East German typewriters, and she had dialed the number: 53348. As she was getting ready to go out, her father glanced up and reminded her that it was the same store at 17 Dupré Street where they had bought electrical appliances in preparation for her married life. But Enayat didn't want any reminders of her marriage. Even the little radio, which she'd owned since she was a girl, had been left behind in Heliopolis.

She stepped through the shop door and fell instantly in love with the Optima. It was beautiful—turquoise, the Arabic letters a pale cream against the black pads of the keys—but what held her attention was the return lever. Previous models had a squat reel, built into the body of the machine; this one was a graceful metal arm lifting from the left side of the carriage and terminating in a turquoise disc.

Through the autumn of 1960 she tried to keep herself as busy as she could while she waited for her divorce to come through and then for her novel to find a publisher, or at least for either Youssef al-Sebaie or Mustafa Mahmoud to get back to her with an opinion about what they'd read. By day she was at the German Archaeological Institute, indexing the library and papers of an Egyptologist by the name of Ludwig Keimer, stepping out onto the balcony to smoke a cigarette with Hilda at twelve thirty.

After work she would come home, first stopping in at her parents' apartment, then taking her son upstairs in the evening. And once he was asleep, she would return to the novel, or read, or talk with Paula or Hilda on the phone. She would try out the new typewriter, tapping keys, setting margins, lifting the slender lever.

But the days her son was with his father, she would feel no desire to go home. She would walk from the German Archaeological Institute on 31 Aboul Feda Street to where her sister Aida worked at the Swiss Antiquities Institute in Gezira Street, overlooking the main branch of the Nile. But instead of taking the direct route, straight across Zamalek, she would exit work and turn right along the smaller branch of the Nile, a stretch of water she had taken to calling "the blind sea" ever since she'd first seen a map of it in Keimer's collection. She would follow the curve of the Corniche as the river widened, walking with the water's edge the length of Gezira Street until she came to her sister. Sometimes she would go straight to Aida's apartment if she was sure that's where she'd be, and then she would take a different route: left into Aboul Feda then left again into Zinki Street, and from there to Shagaret al-Dorr. She might stay over with Aida and her children, particularly if Lt. Col. Anwar Habb al-Rouman was away on army business.

Despite all the information I had managed to gather about Enayat during this period, trying to imagine her as the protagonist in her own life, independent and with agency, Nadia Lutfi's stories kept shifting the picture: Nadia would emerge front and center, her friend Enayat a silhouette passing in the background.

For example, in 1960 Enayat had travelled to Alexandria, her first unaccompanied journey by train, to spend two whole days on set watching Nadia film *Giants of the Seas*. There was the time Nadia signed a contract for *My Only Love* and invited Enayat to a celebratory lunch at Le Grillon on Qasr al-Nil Street. It made Enayat shy, sitting at the same table as the producer Gamal al-Leithy and assorted film stars, and she left early. Three days later, Nadia took Enayat to have supper at the house of the director Ezzeddine Zulfiqar and his wife, Kawthar Shafiq. There was no premature departure that night; in the early hours next morning Enayat was racing with Nadia down the Corniche, and when Nadia returned to her apartment in Bustan Street to sleep, Enayat went straight to work at the institute.

That same year, Enayat placed a call to Nadia's secretary, Rizq, and made a surprise appearance at the Mokattam Casino where Nadia was filming *My Only Love*. It was there that the incident with the handbag took place, what Nadia referred to as "the *raccord* incident."

"So," Nadia explained, "when Enayat called Rizq to find out where I was and turned up at the casino, I was filming a scene where I have to come down a flight of stairs holding a handbag. I borrowed Enayat's bag because it was so beautiful and we shot the scene. When Enayat wanted to leave she asked for her bag back and they told her, No, that won't be possible, there's this thing called *raccord*. Continuity. It had never occurred to her that the bag would have to appear in other scenes and we couldn't do without it. I was supposed to be in a nighttime scene where I danced with Omar al-Sharif. Poor Enayat: she took all her things out of the bag, left it with me, and went off home."

Nadia laughed, and I laughed too.

I sat to watch *My Only Love* on YouTube. I wanted to see the handbag. Thirteen minutes and fifty-five seconds in, Nadia and her lover, Omar al-Sharif, descend the casino stairs. The handbag is in her hand. Omar plays a pilot. Nadia has mistakenly accused him of carrying on an affair with a hostess called Aida, but he has called her on the phone to explain and make up, and now here they are, together again.

"Do you realize how many miles I've covered trying to meet you since I landed?" asks Omar. "From the airport to here, from here to the club, then back here again. And then there's the time I spent flying here from Geneva: that's fifteen hundred nautical miles."

"You count in miles," Nadia replied, "but I count in minutes and moments. Four whole days I've been waiting for you."

Nadia opens Enayat's bag and removes a small tape recorder. Abdel Halim Hafez's "I Love You" starts to play and they begin to dance. And as they dance, Enayat must be walking away from the set without her bag. She might have been asking herself where exactly cinema was finding all this romance. After all, the man who went to war with her over a simple divorce was also a pilot.

By mid-November 1960, Enayat was facing the nightmarish possibility that her husband might summon her to a "house of obedience." Her appeal against the court's rejection of her divorce claim had been turned down.

The court's ruling read as follows:

She is antisocial and does not join her husband and his friends when they come to visit with their eminently respectable families, to share food and drink together. She withholds her company from the marital bed, locking the door of her private chamber and denying her husband what Allah allows. Furthermore, from the contents of a letter (sent from the German Archaeological Institute in Zamalek to the appellant's older sister's residence in Shagaret al-Dorr Street, Zamalek, to ensure that the husband cannot read it) it is clear to the court that the appellant's desire for employment went against her husband's wishes and was obtained without his consent, which he withheld on the grounds that his salary was sufficient to provide her with a comfortable existence, that they had a son to whose care and nurture she should be dedicated and, finally, that her employment was out of keeping with the customs and traditions of the elevated society from which he comes and in which he was raised. At this juncture there was conflict, and on April 7, 1959, the appellant left her marital home in Heliopolis, to which she has so far not returned. Over and above the statements from witnesses, the case documents, and the appellant's own sworn testimony before this court, there is the fact that she went to work at the German Archaeological Institute in 1960 despite her husband's refusal to give his consent for her to take employment.

In other words, in addition to upholding the original judgment, which had rejected her grounds for separation, the court had decided that none of the issues that were the subject of dispute between the couple from September 1959 to October 1960 could be considered either, because they all stemmed from the divorce case itself, and as such, *did not prove that the demand for divorce stemmed from a prior dispute, but rather that all subsequent legal disputes were caused by the initial request for a divorce.* For which reason the court's ruling as regards this appeal was *to reject the appeal, uphold the initial judgment, and order the appellant to meet all costs.*

13.

The personal papers I had seen amounted to just thirteen pages, eleven handwritten and two typed, a grand total of 1,820 words divided between the apartments of Nadia Lutfi and Azima al-Zayyat: all that had survived of Enayat's personal archive, or all that had been permitted to enter wider circulation since the 1960s. Sections of these papers were published less than two months after *Love and Silence* came out. Some were included in Foumil Labib's interview with Nadia Lutfi on May 16, 1967, and the next day Hosn Shah published more in a piece entitled "I Shall Never Die: The Journal of Enayat al-Zayyat." In her introduction to the extracts, Shah writes:

These are pages taken piecemeal from the journal of the young writer Enayat al-Zayyat, author of Love and Silence, *those I was able to find after a sad day spent with her father, Abbas Hilmi al-Zayyat, going through the contents of a box which has remained locked these five years past. This is all that is left of Enayat.*

There are a few passages that have not been published at all. The passages that were have been subjected to only the lightest editorial touch: a title for every paragraph, say, or two smaller paragraphs combined under a single heading; here and there, grammatical corrections. One of the texts that Shah published was taken from the two typewritten sheets, and is in fact a passage from a draft of *Love and Silence*, roughly corresponding to page fifty in the published version.

Among the unpublished pages there are a couple in which Enayat does not talk about herself, does not use *she* or *I*, does not describe death or depression or the prison of marriage, does not touch on her dreams or fears or her relationship with her son. The first of these begins with a name: *Ludwig Keimer*, written in Roman script, followed by notes in Arabic for what could be a short story or chapters of a novel, possibly even a biography, briefly sketched.

On the second, next to the word *friendship* in Arabic the names *Max Meyerhof* and *Paul Kraus* are written in Roman script. There are addresses, too—*17 Youssef al-Guindy Street, The Immobilia Building, 7 Hishmet Pasha Street in Zamalek*— then beneath these, handwritten, a somewhat obscure sentence: *The journey must begin from the tombs.* None of it made sense to me, and the two pages were to remain a mystery until January 2017, when I met Madame al-Nahhas, Enayat's friend and neighbour when she was living in Abdel Fattah al-Zeini Street, who told me that Enayat had started a second book.

It was a novel about the German Archaeological Institute, she said; about "the life of a German man, a botanist who'd come to live in Egypt."

I returned to the plot outlines on the first sheet, and started looking up the names. There was lots in German about Ludwig Keimer, but then I found an article about him in English by a researcher called Isolde Lehnert, and translated it into Arabic. For a good while, this article would contain everything I knew about the man that so obsessed Enayat that she had begun planning to write a book about him:

Giants of Egyptology
—27th of a series—
LUDWIG KEIMER (1892–1957)
by Isolde Lehnert

Ludwig Joseph Gustav Keimer was one of the most prolific Egyptologists to have lived and worked in Egypt. His interests spanned an impressive variety of subjects, although he is best known for his work on Egypt's landscape and environment and how those influenced the thoughts, lives, and religion of the Ancient Egyptians.

In 1957 the German Archaeological Institute Cairo acquired the archives of Keimer, consisting of his former library and scholarly estate. Both reflect the various facets of a scholar who was occupied with subjects ranging from the slightly exotic, in terms of traditional Egyptology (tattooing in Ancient and modern Egypt), to the more Egyptologically conventional. Living and working half of his life in Cairo, he became a kind of institution in academic circles, someone to be consulted regarding almost every Egyptological question.

Ludwig Keimer was born on August 23, 1892, oldest son of a well-to-do landowner and forester in Hellenthal-Blumenthal, a small town in North Rhine—Westphalia, Germany. After finishing school near Hanover, he matriculated to the University of Münster in autumn 1912, to study there a host of subjects: German, history, archaeology, and classical philology. He graduated five years later with a thesis titled "The Greek Thrones from Ancient Times until the Fifth Century BC." In the same year, he went to Berlin to attend lectures in Egyptology by Adolf Erman (1854–1937) and Georg Möller (1876–1921). But this was not the end of his academic studies. Acceding to his father's wishes, he undertook law and economics at Würzburg University, completing the law degree in 1922. Then, continuing in this practical and dutiful vein, two years later at the same institution, he obtained his third doctorate in politics.

But Keimer's real passion was Egyptology, a passion that had intensified since 1918, when he met Georg Schweinfurth (1836–1925), the famous Africa explorer and botanist. Schweinfurth, who was already in his eighties, lived in a house in the midst of Berlin's lush Botanical Garden, and was working on editing his papers for publication. Despite their difference in age, it seems to have been a perfect match from the very beginning. Soon Schweinfurth entrusted the botanical material he had collected in Egypt to Keimer, and instructed him how to proceed with it. Keimer enthusiastically accepted Schweinfurth as his "mentor," and their teamwork yielded rich results, the first being Keimer's book Die Gartenpflanzen des alten Ägypten *[The Garden Plants of Ancient Egypt], published in 1924, with a preface by Schweinfurth. Dealing with forty-four horticultural plants, it remains until today a fundamental work on this topic.*

Keimer enjoyed seven intensive years of collaboration with Schweinfurth, who, according to his correspondence, seemed to have been well pleased with his student. After Schweinfurth's death in 1925, Keimer honored him with several obituaries and compiled a bibliography of his works one year later. After a short collaboration with Victor Loret (1859–1946) in Lyon, France, Keimer followed

Schweinfurth's final words of advice to him: settle in Egypt, a land of immense and inexhaustible possibilities for researchers in almost all branches of the humanities. In the autumn of 1927, Keimer arrived in Cairo, eyes wide open and ready to make his mark in the field of Egyptology.

In Cairo Keimer again followed closely in the footsteps of his teacher, who had lived and worked in Egypt prior to his retirement to Berlin; indeed, by 1928, a mere year after his arrival in Egypt, Keimer had been elected a member of the Société Royale de Géographie d'Égypte, an organisation that Schweinfurth had founded in 1875, upon orders of Khedive Ismail (1830–1895). Keimer's initial years in Cairo were spent as "surveys": he explored his new hometown, strolled around the botanical garden, visited bookshops and antique dealers, and also traveled throughout the country.

This way of engaging with his surroundings continued to characterize Keimer throughout his life. In order to earn a living, he took photographs of the landscape, as well as the monuments, and sold copies to the Belgian Fondation Égyptologique Reine Élisabeth. This arrangement was made with Jean Capart (1877–1947), the foundation's director at that time, who wished to support the promising young scholar.

In 1929 Keimer obtained a two-year position as Professeur à l'École Archéologique des Guides et Dragomans d'Égypte, and then was associated with the Catalogue Général of the Egyptian Museum. These years are scarcely documented. But Keimer's published articles show clearly his focus on flora and fauna and his constant attempt to bridge the gap between Egyptology and the natural sciences. He believed that only a combination of both could enrich the knowledge of Ancient Egypt. In 1931 Keimer got the chance to prove this.

Convinced by a recommendation of Jean Capart, King Fouad I (1868–1936) entrusted Keimer with the organization of the historical section at the newly founded Agricultural Museum, which was inaugurated on January 16, 1938, as the world's first institution of its kind. Being director of the museum's historical section, Keimer was not only responsible for the concept behind the entire exhibition, but also for the acquisition and display of objects.

Besides this task Keimer continued to teach, research, and publish. From 1936 on Keimer was professeur délegué at the Université Fouad Premier, which later became Cairo University, as well as a regular lecturer at Alexandria University. From 1938 to 1939, he was a professor at the German University in Prague, which ultimately gave him Czech citizenship. Already in late 1937 or early in 1938 Keimer had given up his German nationality, to protest the Nazi regime. He reacted to the increasing political tensions in Europe when the Nazis gained control over Germany, with dramatic results not only for Europe but for Egypt as well.

The German residents in Cairo and Alexandria were split, the majority of them supporting one of the strongest sections of the German National Socialist Party abroad. But Keimer was anti-Nazi. He even went one step further in divorcing himself from his native land and culture: he changed his name to Louis and eschewed using German, reverting almost exclusively to French.

Despite his anti-Nazi sentiments, Keimer could not escape the fate of many Germans in Egypt during the Second World War. In 1940 he was detained in an internment camp in or near Cairo by the British military government. Luckily, however, Keimer had friends in high places. Thanks to the interventions of two important men, Keimer was finally released in 1942. One of his champions was the

Egyptologist Walter Bryan Emery (1903–1971), who at that time worked for the British Secret Service; the other was Sir Walter Smart (1883–1962), the Oriental Counselor at the British Embassy. But those terrifying two and a half years must have left indelible traces on Keimer's personality and behavior.

After the war Keimer tried to emigrate to the United States, but without success. So he stayed in Cairo and changed his nationality again in 1951, becoming an Egyptian citizen. Throughout this period, and despite the trials he suffered, Keimer remained active in Egyptology. He played a key role in the renowned Institut d'Égypte, which had been founded by Napoleon in 1798. Keimer became a member of the institute in February 1937, and he ultimately became secretary-general in 1951 and vice president in 1954. Many of his works were published in the institute's Mémoires or in its Bulletin. In addition to being a member of the institute, Keimer was also an active member of other scientific societies and museums in Egypt and abroad. Although some were Egyptological in nature, others were not, and reflected the breadth of Keimer's interests and his knowledge and engagement with his adopted country.

One institution in which Keimer was deeply engaged was the Desert Institute, an Egyptian state-owned research center in Cairo, which granted him an Order of Merit in 1951, for his compilation of an ethnographic collection from Upper Egypt and Nubia. Other ethnographic collections of Keimer went to several institutions in Egypt, including the Geographical Department of Giza University, and abroad. For example in 1951 the Dutch Museum voor Land-en Volkenkunden in Rotterdam received an assemblage of about two hundred and fifty objects from the Bishari and Ababda tribes, which give an insight into their typical clothing, ceramics, basketry, and weapons. Keimer provided a second one, with everyday-life objects from the Beja people, for the Museum für Völkerkunde in Basel, that displayed them in 1957 in a special exhibition entitled Beduinen aus Nordostafrika *[Bedouins of Northeast Africa].*

Keimer had become increasingly interested in combining ethnographic studies with Egyptology, and in using ethnography to elucidate the culture and traditions of the Ancient Egyptians. Although Keimer was by no means the first scholar to do so—indeed, a whole section of the anthropologist Winifred Blackman's book, The Fellahin of Upper Egypt, *is devoted to this—he certainly employed this mode of research to great effect, commenting on tattoos, beekeeping traditions, and other practices and technologies that had continued from Pharaonic Egypt into the modern period.*

Keimer had actively pursued this sort of investigative agenda from the late 1940s onward, a research trajectory which seems to have been influenced by the advice of his mentor, Schweinfurth. Both scholars believed in a cultural continuity between the Ancient Egyptians and contemporary tribes living in the same region, a belief and field of research that continues to this day. Indeed, Keimer discovered such relics among the Bishari, one of two northern Beja tribes living as nomads between the Nile and the Red Sea. He repeatedly visited the Bishari camp close to Aswan, where he carried out his studies. He used paintings of the well-known draughtsman and traveller Joseph Bonomi (1796–1878), or early photographs, for comparing artifacts of both civilizations; and Keimer interviewed Bishari tribespeople, in order to find analogies in their way of living and thinking.

Keimer received more than 90 percent of his information from two old, highly regarded Bishari men, who were also his reliable business partners. The publication of the first results of his travels to the Bishari was destined to be Keimer's last opus. Neither the announced bibliography of the Bishari nor the outcome of his journeys into Sudan in 1952 and 1953 were ever published. Louis Keimer died of cirrhosis of the liver, seven days short of his sixty-fourth birthday, on August 16, 1957, in the Deir el Chifa Hospital in Cairo, thus depriving Egyptology of one of its most unusual and prolific scholars.

As said, shortly before his death, Keimer sold his extensive library and personal archive to the German Archaeological Institute in Cairo. This comprised some seven thousand books, nearly the same number of off-prints, as well as Keimer's photography collection and all of his notes and sketches.

14.

I began my term-long sabbatical in the winter of 2017 and we traveled to Cairo a few days before the New Year. After a pleasant week with family and friends, my son Mourad returned to Boston, my husband flew to Ghana for his research, and I went to the Egyptian National Library to hunt for the texts of nineteenth-century plays. I wanted to know if and how they depicted accents on the page, specifically those of Europeans, Syrians, Greeks, and Jews, and so on. The research was fascinating and life was easygoing and calm. Emerging from the library's archives every afternoon, I would either sit at a café by myself or go home. In the evenings, when I wasn't meeting friends, I would sort through the boxes I had fetched from my father's house and repack their contents into pristine, reinforced cardboard boxes: one for letters, then another for drafts of my earliest poems, then another for my digests of Marxist texts and the books of Tayyeb Tizini, Abdallah Laroui, and Samir Amin. I compiled a file of all the attacks made on the nineties generation of writers in the Egyptian press and couldn't believe how big it was. I brushed the dust from Abdel Moneim Saoudi's gift of the HADITU archive and transcripts of my interviews with its members and placed them in a pile in the living room, to remain there until I could buy a box big enough to hold them. I arranged my journals and diaries in chronological order, starting with year five, primary, all the way through to 1997. My own private archive, I told myself. The thought made me consider just how long I'd been alive: such a long time, so much longer than I'd ever expected. And then it occurred to me that Enayat had owned an archive, too—a little smaller, perhaps, than mine had been at the same age—and that if she really hadn't wanted anyone to see it then she would have burned it before she took those little pink pills.

Through the communist lawyer, I found myself suddenly back in touch with all those who had been part of my life back in the early 1990s, in Cairo. And it occurred to me that my mission to retrieve the boxes from my father's house during Eid, 2015, had come on the heels of my encounter with Azima al-Zayyat and just before my discovery of Astra Square and my first meeting with Nadia; I would never have revisited my archive had it not been for my interest in Enayat. That it was Enayat who'd prompted me to revisit the pain I'd been through during this period of my life, and want to understand it—to make peace with its cast of characters in the present.

It was during this happy period that I received a message from Dr. Kareem Abou al-Magd, director of the center for gut rehabilitation and transplantation at the Cleveland Clinic. He wrote that he would be in Cairo for three days from

January 18 and would be delighted to come and take a look at my sister Amal, about whose health I had contacted him. He gave an endless list of tests which he wanted us to run, and we put him in touch with the Air Force Hospital in the Fifth Settlement district so that he could organize an appointment for the day he was due to fly in. We spent a few days running the gauntlet of tests and doctors, before finally meeting him at the hospital. Amal must go into theater immediately, he decided; her surgery could not be delayed until he returned in July. My younger sister Sanaa and I immediately arranged for the (considerable) fees to be found and transferred; after some deliberation, we agreed not to notify our father in Mansoura until Amal was out of surgery.

I spent most of the next two weeks in hospital. In the evenings, Sanaa would leave her daughters with her husband and come by, and the three of us would sit up together until it was time for me to go back to Manial, while Sanaa slept over. I had never been this close to my sister before. Sanaa was twelve years younger than me and considerably more versed in the ways of Egyptian hospitals and the neglect of their doctors and nurses. Several times a day, she would call to remind me to check Amal's temperature and blood sugar levels, or have a nurse empty the drainage bag, or encourage the patient to get up and move about the room and drink more fluids and so on. Away from the wider family, I was encountering Sanaa's sense of humor for the first time. Her favorite target for mockery was our bizarre family history and she could imitate all the parts required, transforming our tragedies and pains into pure comedy.

We were happy with how well everything was going and the success of the surgery. I was particularly happy, because I was here in Egypt at last: following my sister's endless journey through various medical procedures from another continent had almost driven me mad.

Aida and Azima crossed through my mind all the time. I hadn't treated Azima's pain with sufficient respect, I thought: I should go and see her. And so I did, but this time without a researcher's impatient fixation on stories about Enayat. I wanted to let her know that I understood her. When I saw her, though, I couldn't find the words.

Amal was discharged on the morning of February 11, and on February 13, I went to sign copies of my book *How to Mend: Motherhood and Its Ghosts* at the Townhouse Gallery. Two days later, I spent a wonderful few hours in conversation with students from the School of Translators at Ain Shams University. At this last event, something happened which felt to me like the high point of my trip. One of the students approached me, asking if I'd sign two books: a collection of my poems which had been put out by Makatabat al-Usra, and my book on motherhood.

"Sign the poems for me," she said, "and the other one for my mother. She's your age, and she used to love your poetry, but she's stopped reading." I wasn't overjoyed to hear I was her mother's age, but at the same time I was swept by the emotion that I'd first felt in the summer of 2015. It was the same feeling that had been prompted by my arrival at my father's house the night of Eid, and by the maps of the Land

Survey Administration; it had been present that evening at the Townhouse, during my meetings with Azima and Nadia, and the moment I first entered the street where Enayat had lived. A feeling that I was here.

I was here. The sentence belongs to Enayat. It is in her novel and in her journals, too, in the moments when she doubts her existence will leave any trace at all. As though Enayat, who had died before I was born, was introducing to me a part of my own life, forcing me to reconsider my relationship with the place in which Enayat remained invisible.

Two days after the event at Ain Shams, I was on my way back from Cairo to Boston. My mind was at peace, blithely confident that I could work on the book while taking care of Mourad, then return to Canada in late June and keep writing through July and August until I returned to teaching in September.

I didn't manage a single word of the book for the whole of 2017.

Once back in Boston, I started to read: theoretical texts on accent, some books I'd brought back from Egypt, and novels and plays on Mourad's syllabus that I hadn't read before. My days were spent reading and cooking, and my evenings like a proper mother, sitting with my son as he studied. We had drawn up a schedule of universities he was thinking of applying to and each weekend we would travel down to New York or other cities nearby to visit them. In Canada I spent two months repairing the roof of our house, fixing the windows, painting the walls, and putting in a new kitchen. Whole weeks were spent tossing out anything and everything that I felt was surplus to requirements: kitchen appliances, clothes, the furniture of the bedrooms of two boys who'd left home before they'd reached fifteen.

The words I did write could have been entries in a fantastical journal: a long list of English home-renovation vocabulary which I was learning for the first time, the immigration stories of the laborers who passed through my house, transcripts of my weekly phone calls to Youssef in Utah, Mourad's account of the cancer research he was doing with rats during his internship at MIT, and Michael's stories from Ghana. Nothing about Enayat. Perhaps this was writer's block; maybe it was just a brief shutdown after all those essays about motherhood. Whatever the case, I was content.

September came and my husband returned from Ghana with his study group. I was so pale and had lost so much weight that he took fright and took me straight to the family doctor. I have acute anemia and for the past two months I'd had no kitchen to speak of and no one around to make me eat. The house was a tip, so chaotic that I would make my bed somewhere different every night, wherever there was space amid the furniture and junk. And now I was teaching, too.

My brother Mohammed came on a visit from Beirut and had stayed to oversee the plumbing being put in, the kitchen being installed, the pictures being rehung: everything that turned our house back to a home. At the airport, he told me how upsetting it was to see me in this state, however well I hid it.

Through the autumn of 2017, I was a ghost at the feast, hands trembling round my coffee cup, moods flicking at lightning speed between extremes. Panic attacks were back, descending without warning, and sleeping pills had no effect on my insomnia. Every day was a labored passage through the hours of work, and nights a black hole into which I'd drop despairingly. Worst of all was the return to therapy: an hour with the psychologist every Wednesday.

15.

Early in the summer of 1939, the German freighter *Kairo* put
in at Alexandria, having delivered its cargo to various ports
around the Mediterranean. According to its schedule, it was
due to leave for Hamburg the next day. On arrival, the ship's
cook contacted an officer of the port police called Ismail, and
asked him to deliver an urgent message to the Jewish Hospital
in Alexandria.

Ismail took this in his stride. Both he and the officer
assisting him knew exactly what steps to take in such circumstances. They rushed the letter to Dr. Fritz Katz, chief
surgeon at the hospital, and sat down to await his reply. The
letter read as follows:

*We have a secret human cargo on board this vessel: ten individu-
als, all elderly with the exception of a young mother and her daughter.
The ship's captain has discovered the cargo and to prevent their escape
is placing them under lock and key whenever we put into port. He
is determined to return them to Germany.*

Katz observed the same procedure he had followed on all
previous occasions. Maritime law obliged ships' captains to

inform port authorities if there was any illness aboard their vessels and all disembarkation would have to halt until the sick passengers had undergone a medical examination. Ismail returned to the *Kairo* with sleeping pills and a printed table which calculated dosage according to size and weight, and the cook proceeded to follow Katz's instructions.

A few hours later, a second doctor from the Jewish Hospital arrived at the ship in the company of an official from the port's quarantine authority in order to sign off on the examination of the passengers. All of them were in a deep sleep, with the exception of the little girl, whose mother had refused to give her a pill. Having received permission from the director of quarantine, the Jewish Hospital took charge of the passengers, formally treating them for pleurisy and anemia over the course of two months. And then—as had happened on previous occasions—the older members of the group were transported under guard to the quarantine holding cells in Port Said and there, with the clandestine assistance of a series of Egyptian police officers and officials, they were placed on board a fishing vessel bound for Palestine.

Only Athela, the young mother, and her daughter, Avis, remained in Egypt. Athela had asked to be put in touch with a relative of hers named Herbert, head of the Bata shoe company in Cairo, and Herbert duly arrived in Alexandria and signed for guardianship of his relatives.

"You can read more about the story of how the boat came to Egypt," Avis told me. "An Israeli author wrote a book about the role the Jewish Hospital played in sheltering refugees. I'll send you her name and the title of the book."

I didn't read Hebrew, I told her: no need to trouble yourself.

In 1940, a young girl called Emilia sat crying next to Enayat on their first day at the German kindergarten in Bab al-Louq. Over the phone from her home in Florida, Avis would tell me that she hadn't been crying out of fear; it was that her mother had told her the day before that her name was now Emilia. Emilia Avis. She wasn't Avis any more.

"She was very clear that I mustn't tell anyone, but I was in shock. I didn't understand why this was happening. Enayat and I became friends, and two or three years later I told her that I was actually called Avis, and that I hated the name Emilia, and she started calling me Av-av."

In the garden of the German School, Bab al-Louq, Cairo.
Enayat is at the far left, holding the cat. Her older sister Aida is
also in the picture, seated third from the right in the middle row,
looking at the camera.

In 1950, Av-av and her mother emigrated to America. She never saw Enayat again, but they stayed in touch, mailing each other letters and pictures.

"The last time I wrote to her was after we'd just bought our first house in New Jersey. In '61 or '62 it must have been, because I sent her a photograph of myself and my three children standing outside the front door. I wrote that my oldest daughter didn't care for kindergarten, though the teachers there were so kind and gentle when compared to Sister Ada at the German School. I never heard back."

Av-av worked for years as a nurse at the Children's Specialized Hospital in New Jersey and is now retired and living alone in Florida. She has two grandsons by her youngest daughter, and in 2000 realized a longstanding dream when she returned to Egypt: "I wanted to revisit my childhood. Germany meant nothing to me, so I went to Egypt."

Of all Enayat's classmates and friends from the German School, I was only able to speak to three. So many of the pupils there had been foreigners and had subsequently gone abroad and changed their names after marriage. But luck was on my side when Madame Oun in Cairo gave me Madame Dous's number in Alexandria, and Madame Dous put me on the trail of Emilia. "I never lost touch with Emilia," said Madame Dous. "I was the one who contacted her when Enayat died. When my boy went abroad to study in 1970, he stayed with Emilia for a week. I met her twice in America myself, back when I was still traveling, and I invited her over when she visited Egypt."

Av-av told me: "Enayat didn't sit the German School exams in the summer of 1948. She hadn't wanted to leave her bed since at least the Christmas holidays. She'd have panic attacks, crying fits, then she stopped coming to school altogether and missed out on the exams at the end of June. It was the first time her father realized that his daughter, the daughter he was closest to, wasn't all right."

Had Abbas understood that his daughter was going through a depression?

"I don't know. But he was an enlightened and cultured man and he must have looked into it. He came to the school and they gave him an address and promised that the matter would be treated as confidential. So one morning in February 1948, he turns up at the door of a little German asylum in Maadi."

For the first time I understood why Enayat had been held back a year despite her clear academic excellence.

In autumn of that same year, in that same class, Paula had sat down next to her, and so another friendship began. Had Paula known the reason and decided not to say, or had Enayat kept it to herself? Depression was an old friend, then: it had grown with her from childhood and the moment of her suicide was the final chapter in a long and perhaps ultimately doomed struggle.

The building which housed the asylum is still standing, but when you pass it now you see a garden, a swing, and a little wooden hut, perfect for hide-and-seek; you hear the voices of well-off children at play.

In 1913, the director of the Society of St. Charles Borromeo in Alexandria set aside a small building, next to the society's nunnery and its paupers' hospital, as a residence for nurses in Maadi. At the time, the neighborhood of Maadi was still relatively modest, an unpretentious stop on the Cairo–Helwan line. Helwan itself was one of the most famous resorts in the world, the curative properties of its dry air sought by consumptives, asthmatics, and rheumatics. This residence retained a large garden until the 1980s. It's said there were around seventy trees, palms and pines and fruit trees, alongside birds and animals like ducks, geese, rabbits, and pigs.

In 1914, Britain declared Egypt a protectorate and began to requisition German land and property. The German School in Bab al-Louq, founded by the Society of St. Charles Borromeo in 1904, was closed along with all the German Protestant schools, and most German citizens were expelled from the country. But in Maadi, the Sisters of Mercy of St. Borromeo stayed on: the nunnery, nurses' residence, and paupers' hospital remained open and became a refuge for those nuns who had decided to stay.

With the end of the war in 1918, diplomatic relations between Egypt and Germany were restored, and by late 1921 Germans were permitted to enter the country and reopen the schools.

In 1924 the nurses' residence was converted into a clinic. Initially there were only nine rooms for patients, but the building was renovated and a new wing added, and by 1939 it could house twenty-five. The school in Bab al-Louq remained open through the Second World War—when Enayat studied there, for instance—as did the clinic. When the war ended, Catholic officers and rank-and-file soldiers from Poland, South Africa, and Australia would congregate in the clinic's garden on Sunday afternoons, where they were served tea and biscuits by the sisters.

Wounded German prisoners were also treated here and British priests would distribute food and clothes and books to them. One pair of talented prisoners painted flowers and birds onto the window panes, designs that can be seen from the street to this day.

The clinic shut its doors in 1964. Most of the sisters were by now too old to work there and they had trouble attracting young women from Germany to join their mission. But unmarried teachers at the German School had been in need of a residence since the beautiful villa next to the school, which had housed them since 1929, was demolished in 1960. The school had first rented a building for them in Maadi, but it proved too small to meet the demand for rooms, and in the end these difficulties and others were solved by the stroke of a pen: the school decided to convert the clinic in Maadi into a kindergarten, nursery, and teachers' residence, while setting aside a wing to house the nine nuns who had worked at the clinic: three of them were over eighty years old, five over sixty, and there was a single young woman called Claudia.

When I visited the building in February 2019, only Claudia was left. She was ninety, cared for by nuns on secondment from Assiut, who called her Mama.

From 1934 onwards, the clinic had specialized in treating what was referred to as *madness*. The sisters were overseen by Mother Arsenia. In 1948, the number of beds was increased still further, to forty. Dr. Maurice Gelat stayed on as director of the clinic until his death in 1946, when he was replaced by his assistant, Dr. Antoin Arab.

Dr. Arab was said to be a fervent believer that medicine never stood still, and would spend a month every summer in Switzerland, acquainting himself with the latest treatments. The year he took over the clinic, legislation was issued placing all psychiatric institutions under state control, but Dr. Arab managed to preserve the European nature of his establishment; people would say it felt like a retreat in the Swiss countryside. Patients from the German community continued to use its services, along with those Egyptian families who shared the view that modern medicine treated not just the body but the soul as well.

The majority of the patients were women and hysteria was the most common diagnosis. Dr. Arab also happened to be a priest, and a reasonable one at that. After Enayat had been under observation at the clinic for five weeks, he decided that staying on in the company of these older "hysterics" would not help her improve. He advised Abbas to take his young daughter to what was then the best hospital in the region.

Enayat's relationship with the Behman Hospital began in 1948. She was to visit it for the last time in November 1962.

16.

In 1940, on a slight rise in Helwan, Benjamin Behman founded the first specialist psychiatric hospital in the region. Born in Assiut in the south of Egypt, Behman completed his studies in London in 1918, and returned to Cairo to practice medicine. In 1922 he joined the staff at the Abbasiya Asylum, popularly known as the Yellow Palace, a phrase that was later to become synonymous with mental illness in Egyptian slang. There, he worked under the superintendent of the asylum, Dr. John Warnock, then his successor, Dr. Herbert Dudgeon.

He learned a great deal from the experience. Like the Medico-Psychological Association in London, the British community in Egypt, and King Fouad himself, Behman fully recognized Dr. Warnock's role in establishing a system of modern psychiatric treatment in Egypt. When Warnock had arrived in the country in 1895, the Abbasiya Asylum had been in a wretched state.

The building had begun life as the Red Palace, a residence for a member of the Khedive's family. A serious fire had destroyed much of the main building and left the quarters of the Ethiopian maids and the stable block untouched, to which quarters the Egyptian government had transferred patients from the Boulaq Hospital in 1880 at the urging of the British commissioner. Despite renovations to what remained of the Red Palace, Warnock was shocked by its condition as a place of medical treatment. Doctors were living over three miles away in central Cairo, leaving the patients in the care of their assistants and staff, and there seemed to be no barrier to practicing there: among their number was an Italian conman who had never formally studied medicine and was using forged papers. Becoming a patient was equally frictionless. All it took was a letter from the police bearing your name, with no medical examination required. Furthermore, the annual mortality rate among residents was 23 percent, and postmortems revealed high numbers of bone fractures and severe breakages as a result of rough handling when being restrained. The ruins of the main building housed the hospital's three hundred male patients, while 130 women were accommodated in the stable block next door.

It wasn't all bad, however. Patients ate well and morale was high among a nursing staff who were not held legally responsible for any deaths or pregnancies on their wards.

Over the course of the next twenty-six years Warnock modernized every aspect of the institution, recruiting fifteen Egyptians from the military hospital and drawing up a number of laws and regulations, including punishments for staff in cases of neglect and measures to assist female patients who fell pregnant. He also banned patients from leaving the grounds to receive blessings at saints' shrines as they would sometimes escape or become involved in public disturbances. One wing of the stable block was converted into a residence for female patients, and he installed a kitchen, bakery, and laundry, as well as laying out shaded walkways for the patients and planting trees. The sewage system was upgraded, eliminating the foul odors that had permeated the establishment. Patients were allotted to one of six wards depending on the severity of their condition, and a system was instituted to prepare those due for release, with the opportunity to learn basic crafts and trades.

By 1923—that is, one year into Benjamin Behman's time at the Yellow Palace—the number of staff had grown from the 73 recorded in 1895, to 698, while that of the patients had swelled from 465 to 2,472 over the same period: evidence, albeit superficial, of Warnock's pet theory that the more "civilized" a people became, the more prone they were to insanity. In his view, Egyptians were making great strides.

Warnock also contributed to theories of a predisposition to madness in hot climates. In reports sent to *Brain: A Journal of Neurology* Warnock stated that in men, more than 30 percent of cases of insanity were caused by hashish; in women, the principal cause was said to be sex. Warnock became a consultant to the French occupation in North Africa and colonial administrators in India and the Far East. But Behman was unpersuaded by his theories and unsympathetic to the systems in operation both in Abbasiya and at the Khanka Hospital, which Warnock had founded in 1911 and which classified patients and treated them according to how "civilized" they were. Here, one set of regulations applied to English patients, a second to Egyptians from wealthy families, a third to those from the professional classes, and a fourth to the poor. Furthermore, despite Warnock's efforts and improvements, the hospital's facilities and standards fell short of those Behman had seen in England.

Behman's dream was to establish a psychiatric hospital that would meet international standards, and this he was able to accomplish in partnership with Durham University. A doctor from the World Health Organization, who inspected it in 1959, praised the hospital for incorporating the latest advances in psychiatric medicine and for its use of insulin treatments.

I had wanted to visit the Behman Hospital in the summer of 2018, but it was only later that year, back in Cairo for a week in November, that I was able to go. I made an appointment with Dr. Nasser Loza, director of the hospital and the grandson of Behman and his wife, the surrealist artist Julienne Fagard. On Thursday, November 15, 2018, he welcomed me into his office and listened as I questioned him about the medicines and treatments that would have been used on psychiatric patients in the period from the late 1940s to January 1963.

"The number of drugs available was very limited," he explained. "A doctor would try them on himself before prescribing them to patients. Things have changed, of course. If a doctor sampled all the drugs he was dispensing, he'd go mad himself. There were three standard treatments for psychiatric patients at that time. The first was pharmaceutical: Imipramine and Tofranil are antidepressants and antianxiety drugs; they speed up the metabolism, increase appetite, and restore some of the patient's interest in daily life.

"The second approach was abreaction—or speech—therapy, with its roots in Freudian analysis. Freud's studies of hysteria pay particular attention to the concept of suppressed emotions and desires, and associate this suppression with trauma. The idea is to liberate these emotions by reaching back to the moment to which they are unconsciously coupled. Jung was skeptical of the centrality of residual trauma to psychological disturbance. He regarded trauma as a delusion, or invention, of the patient.

"During the period you're interested in there was a third addition to this range of treatments: insulin. Patients were given injections of insulin. The dose of insulin went straight into the vein, making the patient feel dizzy; then they were given sugar and felt better. And while this was happening they were encouraged to talk to their analysts about their childhoods, their relationships with their mothers, their lives in general."

I asked him about sleeping pills. What pills were being sold in Egypt in the early 1960s? I particularly wanted to know about rose or pink pills sold in packets of twenty.

"You might be talking about the medicine marketed as Veronal," he said. "Named for the serene beauty of the Italian city of Verona, apparently! It contained phenobarbital, which is used to treat insomnia, nervous disorders, and withdrawal."

As our meeting drew to a close, Dr. Loza told me that he was collecting his grandmother's art for an exhibition at the Belgian Embassy in Cairo. I asked him if I could see the archive that he was hoping to turn into a museum about the hospital, and he said, "Of course!" then added, "But there's only books and equipment and drugs, I'm afraid. The hospital doesn't divulge details about its patients, even fifty years on. If you want information about a former patient you'll have to go to the National Mental Health Council and get their permission to view the file in our archive."

"I don't want to see any medical files," I replied.

Standing in the garden outside the archive, waiting for a man to fetch the key and open up, I looked up *phenobarbital* on my phone:

Barbiturates are a class of medicine that affect the central nervous system, producing a wide spectrum of effects, from mild tranquilization to full anesthesia. They were first synthesized in 1864 by German chemist Adolf von Baeyer, and in 1904 it was discovered that they helped dogs sleep. The Baeyer Company took out a patent for tranquilizers whose side effects included listlessness, difficulty concentrating, shortness of breath, and a loss of balance. Overdoses can lead to coma or death.

Germans. So many Germans in Enayat's life.

In November 1962, Enayat paid her final visit to the Behman Hospital: this visit was the thing that Nadia and Azima would not tell me, and the thing that Madam al-Nahhas would.

In the weeks leading up to the visit, Enayat had felt like a ghost at the feast, hands trembling round her coffee cup, mood switching at lightning speed between extremes. Her panic attacks returned, descending without warning, and sleeping pills had no effect on her insomnia. Every day was a labored passage through the hours of work, and nights were a black hole into which she'd drop without hope. Worst of all was going back into therapy: an hour with the psychologist every Wednesday.

That autumn, Enayat made this entry in her journal:

Wretched beauty: death's silent field, the earth unfeeling, a cold that flows between the roses. And the life that passes and the death that's born. In Alexandria, my mind has shown me things I once saw with my eyes and old phrases have sounded in my ears. I have seen people wearing clothes I've seen before . . . but where? I don't know. A barrier in my memory has melted and two lives have run together, yet I still don't know what tomorrow will bring. If tomorrow wanted, it could lift my living body off night's and bring me to it, to the worn-out pages of the day to come. I feel alienated from it all. My eyes are windows, from which I look out at the people and places around me. But I do not touch them: just like that, I am cut off from my life, outside myself, watching and listening as though I, this living, moving body, is nothing to do with me. It feels as though I've already lived this life, so why am I back here again? Glancing at the door, I search for some trace of this former life, but all I can see is an image of stone stairs. So I turn and descend, onwards into a future already lived.

In the archive that was to become a museum were shelves of psychiatric texts in English, French, and German. There were ledgers for the hospital's accounts, but I wasn't permitted to open them. I remembered reading somewhere that in 1948 the amount a patient was required to deposit with the hospital prior to entry had been increased from seven to fifteen pounds. Patients of all nationalities. I tried to picture how the place must have looked in 1948, then in 1962; though some of the European-style buildings and the garden in the old pictures were still recognizable today, much had changed.

Here were the old switchboards. One from the 1940s, another from the 1960s. The former must have been one of the first things Enayat laid her eyes on when she came here in 1948. Visitors were required to wait in a room to the left of the main entrance, in the presence of a security guard, a receptionist, and a switchboard operator whose fingers floated over the blue, red, and green of the button bank, a receiver clamped to one ear.

After meeting the doctor, Enayat was told that she would be staying there for a few days. Anywhere up to a week. A nurse took her to her room: bed, cupboard, and a window which looked out over the garden and part of another building. There was a telephone, too, incoming calls only. The nurse opened the cupboard and showed her a towel and a set of clothes. Everything was printed with the room number, she explained. *No. 28.* Her father would drop off more clothes tomorrow.

Like she was in another country. She would dream of this room frequently thereafter, for the rest of her life in fact, and every time she woke from the dream it would feel as though she had returned from a journey overseas.

A machine for administering shocks. Emergency medical kits in metal cases. Medical instruments whose function eluded me.

A glass display case of medicines. I spotted strips of blue Ritalin tablets, marked CIBA, then my eye fell on the little bottle of Veronal beside it. I asked the attendant if he could open the case for me. *Twenty tablets*, read the label. There was a warning against taking them without a prescription. Then, because Allah knew that I was here for Enayat, there was this: *Expires January 1963.* I unscrewed the lid and peered at the little pink pills inside.

17.

On July 19, 2018, I posted to Facebook asking for assistance in finding a tomb in the Basateen cemetery.

The replies and messages came in, some joking, some suggesting antiquities experts and historians to contact. And then Mohammed Ezzeldin wrote. He was a doctoral student at CUNY in New York, known as Saeed to his friends. I had first met Mohammed in 2015, when he had asked me if I had any material on Arwa Saleh, the communist activist and writer who committed suicide in 1997, and the Egyptian literary scene during the nineties. I had given him some texts which he scanned and returned. I next saw him in May 2017, at a reading of mine in New York, and we had remained in touch ever since. And now he wrote:

I'm in Cairo. Send me your number. There's a researcher called Youssef Osama who knows the cemeteries inside out. Every Friday he does a guided tour for Egyptians around Fatimid Cairo. I've been with him to the graveyards of al-Suyuti and Imam al-Shafie. He's got a page on Facebook called "The Mamluks."

Saeed and Youssef Osama and I exchanged dozens of messages. Seeing that I was going to Beirut and would be back on the evening of June 29, and since Saeed lived nearby, we decided that we would all meet up in Manial on Saturday, June 30, and set off together to hunt down the tomb of Ahmed Pasha Rashid.

On the day appointed, I arrived outside the Faten Hamama Cinema at ten in the morning, to find laborers ripping out the cinema's window frames and doors and battering at the walls with sledgehammers. I thought of Sargon Boulos's poem, "Elegy to Cinema Sinbad," and went to sit on the wall overlooking the Nile to keep clear of the dust. By ten thirty, with the smell of grilled fish starting to drift down from Restaurant Bahrain, there was still no sign of Saeed or Youssef Osama. Saeed's phone was off and Youssef's was engaged. I went through our messages again to check I had the date right, then crossed Roda Street to the café at the intersection with Dar al-Sanaa Street, said to be opposite the building where actress Soad Hosny had lived for a while. I thought about Soad, trying to fight back my growing suspicion that no one was going to show. It was summer, after all: maybe they were both still in bed. At eleven, Youssef called to say that he was with a friend, and that they were on their way to Mohandiseen to pick up a Dr. Sadeq from his apartment. I tried to stay calm. What friend? And who was Dr. Sadeq? I thought we were supposed to be working. Hadn't we agreed that we'd start early in order to beat the heat?

Youssef was in high spirits, chuckling as he spoke: "We'll be there in no time. Drink your tea and relax."

I turned back to my tea, and waited.

At last, Saeed appeared and ordered a coffee. Still half asleep but in a fine mood. "Living abroad has spoiled you," he said. "Nothing happens at ten thirty in the morning here, as you should know. You're lucky, by the way. I know Dr. Sadeq. He knows more about Mamluk and Fatimid cemeteries than anyone in the country."

The sun, as they say, was in the heart of the sky by the time Saeed and I, at last, joined Youssef in the back of the car. "Yousra insisted she bring her car down from Fifth Settlement to spare you the heat. She wants to meet you." So Yousra and I introduced ourselves. A strikingly beautiful young woman who worked as a teaching assistant in the German Department at Cairo University, she was friends with the writer Yasser Abdellatif and read poetry.

Dr. Mustafa Sadeq was a professor of gynecology and obstetrics at Cairo University and head of the infertility and assisted conception unit at the Qasr al-Aini teaching hospital. Which Ahmed Pasha Rashid was I after, he wanted to know. He knew two. Did I mean the Minister of Finance and Public Works under Khedive Ismail? And why? What did Enayat have to do with him? Who was Enayat anyway? His wife's aunt, Tante Nana, was connected to the family by marriage. I showed him a copy of the clipping from *al-Ahram*'s deaths column. This was the only clue I had, I said. This was all I knew. This tomb was all I wanted.

We were passing through downtown when he turned to Yousra and declared: "It's on the highway to the Mamluk cemetery. Al-Afifi Street is the one that runs directly behind the Effendina Mausoleum."

In less than half an hour we were on al-Afifi. We parked next to the brown shell of a car chassis, its tires and windows missing. Three or four kids were playing in the stripped interior. We turned right down al-Afifi and in seconds my companions were crowing in delight. I followed their gaze: a yellow-painted brick wall, surmounted by the long, feathery, intensely green leaves of a tree which rose up from behind it like a tent. Set in the wall was a green sheet-metal door decorated with a regular geometric design, and above this door a plaque, lettered in white and bearing a Quranic verse alongside the words *The Tomb of Ahmed Pasha Rashid*.

I stood behind the others, drunk-feeling, guessing at the name of the tree with the long feathered leaves as though I were here for the botany. Dr. Sadeq rapped at the gate and called, "Ye of Allah!" A few minutes went by, then a man who seemed to be the guard stepped out: a man in his forties wearing a gallabeya and glasses. Before greeting us he carefully locked the gate behind him, as though departing the scene of a crime. Solemn and decorous, Dr. Sadeq asked if we might enter and view the grave of Mrs. Enayat al-Zayyat, to which the man replied with confidence that she wasn't buried here but in the tomb next door. We followed him, and he started fumbling at the lock of a gate which bore the legend: *Courtyard of the Heirs of Benba and Ziba Khatoun, wives of the Amir, Sulayman Agha al-Silahdar, as recorded at the office of the notary public, AH 1278*. I asked the guard if we could go back to the Rashid family tomb, and he refused. "Enayat's not here," I whispered to Dr. Sadeq: "She's in the tomb he came out of. This is a waste of time. There's a family connection between the Rashids and the family of al-Silahdar, but she's not here."

"I know," he said: "I know, just be patient."

We spent a while wandering around the tomb of the Silahdars: the courtyard with locked rooms on the walls which faced you as you entered, and to the right, cactus and acacia everywhere, and more than twenty graves, each the height of a single course of bricks and marked at one end by a modest gravestone, brick again, and cased with cement into which the name of the deceased and the date of burial were carved. Not one of them a Rashid or a Silahdar. Dr. Sadeq explained that the family which owned a plot usually interred its members in the main burial chambers, while courts and yards and side rooms were offered as charitable burial sites to poor relatives or those who had served the family in life, either working their land or as domestic servants. On edge, I tried to calm myself by thinking about the acacia trees. Called *sant* in Arabic, I remembered reading somewhere that they were *shenet* in Ancient Egyptian; that the Ancient Egyptians wove garlands from their flowers and constructed doors and coffins and ships from their wood.

I couldn't believe that we were still standing here with Enayat lying just meters away.

Dr. Sadeq took the guard to one side and seemed to be persuading him to take us to the tombs. When they had finished conferring he introduced us to the man, as though we were meeting him for the first time: "Al-Hagg Hamdan is an upstanding man and will take us to see Enayat."

I wanted to kiss the man's hand, but Dr. Sadeq beat me to it, lacing his arm through Hamdan's and walking on as though he'd known him for years.

The tomb of Ahmed Pasha Rashid

As my companions wandered towards the two big burial chambers facing the entrance, I slowed to read the names on the paupers' burials in the courtyard and fell behind. My heart was beating loud enough to hear. I tried to master the faint tremor in my hands. They emerged from the main chambers—she wasn't in there—and, keeping together, made for a small room to my right. A moment's silence, then Dr. Sadeq was shouting:

"I've found her! Come, Iman! Enayat's in here."

For a long minute I stood there in the courtyard, unable to move her way. I heard their voices and I saw their cameras flash. They were calling to me.

To the right of Enayat's imposing headstone old planks resolved themselves into a storeroom door; between them I could see a bed frame. On the left was an unmarked stone. Behind it was the tomb of Mrs. Zeinab Hanim Rashid, who died on August 19, 1939: the daughter of Ahmed Bek Rashid (son of Ahmed Pasha Rashid) and mother of Enayat's mother, Fahima Ali Abbas. Alongside Zeinab, in a tomb of the same length, lay the remains of a boy, born on November 26, 1933, who died on November 2, 1942. His name is Adel Hussain Wahbe.

Behind me, low beneath the room's small window and without a marble headstone to match the rest, lay a modest grave, and set atop it, the following items: a handsaw, a chisel, pincers, a plane, a hammer, a pair of screwdrivers (one huge, one very small), a steel ruler, a pot of glue, and nails of all sizes. Scratched into the cement, I read the names of the two men who lay beneath this impromptu carpenter's bench, imagining them wide-eyed in the dark, enjoying the saw's rasp, the thud of nails being hammered home. Beneath the wooden frame of the window that overlooked the yard outside lay the grimy hulk of a car chassis full of holes, and beside that, a plastic bucket and an oil rag.

I turned back to Enayat. Yousra held out a tissue and I realized that I was crying, that my chest and neck were wet with tears. It wasn't grief. To be standing there in front of her headstone was the high point of our relationship. The tomb wasn't just another detail, another catalyst to help me reconstruct her unrealized dreams, her sleeplessness, her pain; the tomb was the only place where she actually was. For her life, I had to return to the archive, to the memories of the living, and my own imagination, but I felt now that at last she trusted me, that she had allowed me to reach her along a chain of chance and speculation.

I looked over at my companions: Saeed, with his research into Arwa Saleh and the nineties generation of writers; Youssef Osama, obsessed with Mamluk history and its architectural legacy; Yousra, teaching German to undergraduates. And Dr. Sadeq. In the early 1990s he had been a student in Paris. Every day he would take a map or guide book and ride his bicycle around a neighborhood, checking street names, pulling up before public buildings and reading about them. He often asked himself why we were never taught about this, about the environment in which we lived and died, and since returning to Egypt he had spent his spare time in the sprawling Mamluk burial grounds, compiling data about each and every tomb with a view to some day writing their histories. These companions, I felt, were Enayat's gift to me. I dabbed my eyes, and with the same tissue, wiped at a corner of her headstone, a little patch to make the marble shine.

I heard Yousra whisper to the others that we should be leaving, and so we walked out and went to the Effendina Mausoleum. A high, domed ceiling, red and blue stained glass, glowing marble and carved ivory, Arabic script and worked columns: I stretched out over its carpets and slept, though part of me was still present, listening intently as my friends discussed first the khedives—Tawfiq and Ismail and Abbas II—then moved on to Amina Hanim Ilhami and Princess Fathiya, then the Touson family, then Prince Mohammed Ali, who owned the palace in Manial. Gesturing at a dark patch on the wall, Dr. Sadeq told us the story of how the kiswa—the cloth coverings of the Kaaba which once were kept here—were stolen by a thief who had cut himself as he pulled them free, and his bloodstains had been left on the wall as a warning to others.

I could hear everything that was being said around me but also, somehow, I was dreaming. For a reason known only to Allah, it wasn't Enayat who came to me then, but another woman whose life I'd often thought about. As I lay there, the actress Magda al-Khatib came and sat down beside me. She was young in the dream, as beautiful as she'd been in life, and wearing a black evening dress. As she stretched her legs out, I saw her shoes, deep red with a bow, high-heeled and pointed. In her left hand she held a glass of red wine, while from her right extended a slender cigarette in a long holder. It was like we'd known each other forever.

"Get up, lazy," she said, and laughed tipsily.

I sat up and looked around, trying to understand where I was. My companions were milling around and I called over that we needed to eat. I was hungry and I wanted to be walking. I wanted to go to al-Hussein.

Early the next day I returned to Enayat's tomb. Alone this time, bringing flowers. I spent a while roaming the rooms and trying to puzzle out the family tree. It was a maternal line, a tree of mothers, but in this little side chamber Enayat had no company from her mother's family except her grandmother, who had been buried in 1939, three years after she had been born. It seemed strange that the tomb adjoining hers should

At Enayat's grave

have no name on it, despite having a marble headstone; that she and her grandmother should be buried here, in this out-of-the-way room where most of the graves were for paupers. I wondered if she felt out of place. Her parents were buried with the al-Zayyats and her sister Aida with the Habb al-Roumans; her only child lay with his father, and Azima wanted to be with the al-Sadr family. It was as though her burial was an extension of her writing life: erased from one side of her family tree, an outcast on the other.

I promised her that I would come and visit her whenever I came back to Egypt, and I was sure it was a promise I would keep.

18.

I now resumed my search for the fourth Rashid: Ahmed Pasha
Rashid, variously governor of Cairo, Interior Minister, and
Speaker of Parliament under Khedive Ismail. I found an English-
language site that allowed me to trace his family tree from the
nineteenth century to the present day. In the course of a long
and eventful life, Ahmed Pasha Rashid had married a total of
five times—two Turks, a pair of Egyptians, and an Ethiopian—
and up until the 1940s his family was related through marriage
to Egyptian and Turkish aristocracy, families such as Manastirly,
Taymour, Aoun, Mazloum, al-Tahery, and others. A long
lineage of pashas and beys, ministers and ambassadors, and
nobodies. A good number of Rashid Pasha's descendants left
the country in the wake of 1952, scattering across the globe,
and foreign wives begin to enter the record, with French and
American names predominating in the last two generations. All
well and good. What troubled me was that the names of Enayat
al-Zayyat and her sisters appeared nowhere on the site.

I turned to David, the young man who provides technical
assistance to teaching staff at my university, and asked him to

recommend a program for recording genealogical data. With the program installed, I started to enter the names, next to each the date of death which I had culled from the tomb. And I found an error: the family tree which I'd found online stated that Zeinab Rashid (d. 1939) had married Abbas al-Zayyat, and that their daughters were Fahima, Munira, and Tafida. In other words, the name of her daughter's husband, Abbas al-Zayyat, had been substituted in place of her own spouse: Ali Abbas, an Egyptian-born Turk. One error had led to another: Abbas al-Zayyat's reassignment meant that the names of his actual daughters—Aida, Enayat, and Azima—were lost altogether. Returning Enayat to the family tree meant correcting these mistakes.

I wrote a letter detailing the issues to the email address on the website, though without any real expectation of a reply; the site hadn't been updated for years and it didn't bode well that, in 2018, I was writing to a Yahoo address. Never mind. It had begun to dawn on me that I wasn't fully in control of myself. I was writing these long emails and sending them out the way some people put a message in a bottle and cast it into the sea: not because they want it to be found, but because they will do anything they can to sleep.

I distracted myself by sketching out a second diagram, this one describing the relationship of the Rashid family to the Egyptian intelligentsia. For the first time I was able to make sense of what I had heard about the relationship that connected the writers Mohammed and Mahmoud Taymour to Enayat: they were also grandchildren of Rashid Pasha through their mother. The composer and compiler of Egyptian folklore, Bahiga Hanim, and her younger sister, the author Jadhibiyah Sidqi, were daughters of a minister of works, Mahmoud Pasha Sidqi, but were also related to Enayat's mother's family. I paused over Jadhibiyah. She was the author of *Son of the Nile*, an absurd book with a grim cover that had been forced on my generation in year six. It tells the story of a young orphan, Hamdan, who inherits the trade of fisherman from his dead father and is the embodiment of the model citizen: he helps his community during a drought, landing fish, gathering hay, and sleeping contentedly in his rude hut.

A second book is set in America, and its protagonist is Jadhibiyah herself. She is a paragon of Egyptian womanhood, faultlessly negotiating life in the West. She is eloquent, elegant, and a passionate advocate of Arab causes. Had Jadhibiyah ever heard of Enayat, or had the multiplicity of grandmothers kept Rashid Pasha's granddaughters in ignorance of one another? I dreamed a scene: Enayat meeting Jadhibiyah at a family function, let's say in 1962. The former divorced, living with her father and awaiting the publication of her first novel, and the latter—who has no idea who the first is beyond being a member of the family—a published author in her own right and the wife of Mr. Youssef Zaki, public overseer of subsidized food supplies in Cairo. Jadhibiyah is talking animatedly about her latest book, and about America—how her defense of the High Dam project silenced the Americans she met—while Enayat, who has dreamed her whole life of other lands but has never set foot outside Egypt, stares up at the ceiling, bored.

To my surprise, the very next day I received a reply from Hassan Rashid, administrator of the website. My request seemed to have upset him: *There is no Enayat al-Zayyat in our family. Clearly, the guard at the tomb has been selling grave plots without our knowledge to people who have no relationship to Rashid Pasha. I'd be interested to know just how this has happened.*

I wrote back to say that Enayat had been interred there in 1963, before the current guard was born, and that she wasn't in one of the main burial chambers, but in a side room which, aside from her grandmother Zeinab Rashid, housed charitable burials. I attached the pictures I'd taken to prove that she really was a member of the family, that there wasn't some trick being played, and after some further back-and-forth, we arranged to talk by phone.

Hassan Rashid son of Ahmed Adel Rashid son of Hassan Ahmed Rashid son of Ahmed Pasha Rashid. A man with an American mother and American kids. He had been an environmental scientist with a number of published studies to his name and also written several historical novels and a collection of children's stories, available on Amazon. Hassan lived in Oregon, a pensioner but still active; he gave lectures, wrote fiction, self-published his books and traced the genealogy of the Rashid family. Now here he was, in my life, opening another hole in the wall behind which Enayat lay. He hadn't known she'd ever lived, let alone been buried in the tomb, but even so it seemed to me that this omission of Enayat from the family tree was significant.

"I published a novel, a work of historical fiction that narrated the journey of my great-grandfather, Ahmed Pasha

Rashid, from Greece to Egypt. I went back to the old documents and oral history, but there were gaps I had to fill in for myself. I'll tell you what's known for certain:

"Ahmed Pasha Rashid was once a Greek boy called Dimitri Panzaris. The Turks abducted him during the war in 1822 when he was just six years old, and he became the property of Ahmet Agha al-Khawalli, governor of Kavala. That same year, the Agha was summoned to Egypt by Mohammed Ali, who wanted his assistance building a modern army. Dimitri was the same age as Hassan Shaaban, the Agha's son, so he was brought along to be the boy's companion.

"Dimitri was freed when he turned eighteen and he changed his name to Ahmed Rashid. The man who'd abducted him and handed him to al-Khawalli was called Rashid, so maybe that's why he chose the name. But as for how this slave became a man of great wealth and a minister several times over, well . . . He received an excellent education and could speak several languages, and he also mixed with Mohammed Ali's family and had friends at the heart of political life and high society in Egypt and Turkey.

"In my book, I never talk about his wives or his descendants. Just him. About how he went back to Greece to find his family after he was freed. You won't find any mention of the fact that we are descended from him through his Ethiopian wife, the last woman he married, when he was in his eighties. She was a slave, too. He married her in the Hijaz while on pilgrimage, then brought her back to Egypt. That's why we've never been accepted into the family. My grandfather—and my father and uncle after him—never had anything to do with the

Rashid family. We grew up much closer to my paternal grand-mother's family, the family of Sidqi Pasha which was descended from the family of the very Ahmet Agha al-Khawalli who had bought and then freed Ahmed Pasha Rashid.

"Just so you understand how we stand with the family: my great-grandmother, the Ethiopian, wasn't buried with Ahmed Pasha Rashid's other wives in the main chamber, but in a smaller room with an unmarked headstone, the way they used to do for slaves."

I told him that Enayat had been buried in the Rashid family tomb because her death had been so sudden, and that her father didn't own a burial plot in Cairo; that she was buried directly alongside his Ethiopian great-grandmother and her unmarked marble headstone. I nearly said that all the rejects had been put in that little room with the strangers.

Then Hassan said: "The only descendants of Rashid Pasha that I know about come through his Ethiopian wife. My mother's American. She left Egypt in 1967 and took us back home with her. My father, Ahmed Adel Rashid, worked for the United Nations and we only saw him during the holidays. Always away in Africa: Sudan, Kenya, Ghana, all over. I speak Arabic because I was seventeen when I left Egypt. I've got a brother called Salah Eddin who lives in St. Louis and two sisters: Esmet, who lives close to me in Oregon, and Aida, who's in Egypt. Esmet mapped out the family tree of Sidqi Pasha—that's my paternal grandmother's family—but she doesn't know anything about the Rashid family."

Hassan was answering questions I hadn't even thought to ask him: Why hadn't Enayat turned to Bahiga Sidqi Rashid or her sister Jadhibiyah when she was having difficulties publishing her novel?

"If Enayat really was a member of the family, as you say, she certainly wasn't close to either of them. Our branch had nothing to do with the rest of the Rashids. I drew the tree based on the archives of the waqf and a few things my cousin Hani had come across in Egypt. When my great-grandfather died, his son, Hassan Bek Rashid, was just three years old. Abdel Hamid Pasha Sadeq raised the child as his ward, and when he passed away in turn, Hassan Rashid was taken in by Mahmoud Pasha Sidqi. He became an engineer and a composer, then married his guardian's daughter, Bahiga, who was known as Bahiga Rashid Sidqi, or sometimes Bahiga Sidqi Rashid. Bahiga was born in 1900 and graduated from the American College for Girls in 1919. She was a musician and folklorist and author of *Egyptian Folk Songs*, which was published in 1958. At one point she was president of the Hoda Shaarawy Society and participated in many conferences on women's issues overseas. She died on October 6, 1987.

"Now the family of Hassan Shaaban al-Khawalli, his son Abdel Hamid Pasha Sadeq, and all their descendants, they're our real family. Plus the Rashid girls who married back into it, like Zeinab Rashid, who married my grandmother's brother, Ahmed Mahmoud Sidqi. We call her Tante Raana. She had so much money that after her husband died she decided to live in a hotel to spare herself the trouble of managing a household and staff.

"We lived in a big house facing the mausoleum of Saad Zaghloul, which had been divided in two: one part became the Amun Language School, and the second, which was by no means small, housed my grandfather Hassan, my uncle, and my immediate family. In the early sixties, we built a villa at the intersection of 218 Street and 206 Street in Maadi and moved there. It's still standing today."

The first call ended with Hassan Rashid pledging to look into the question of Enayat's relationship to the Rashid family. He gave me the number of his cousin Hani, seventy-four years old and living in 6th of October City, then said that he'd be coming to Egypt in April 2019, and intended to visit the tomb with Hani before making any corrections to the family tree.

Though I had been eager at first to see Enayat restored to her mother's family, I now began to think of her exclusion as purely serendipitous: an error that carried none of the literary, ideological, or gender bias which had knocked her off the family tree of literary and cultural relationships in Egypt, an error that was more like a forgetting, one with its own beauty. And maybe she would want herself to remain that way, on the outside.

19.

Mohammed Samaka was the first person I spoke to when I came to Sherbiny Street in Dokki, the summer of 2015. He gave up his own time to show me around, and introduced me to Ghannam, who he described as the oldest resident in the street. Ghannam was seventy-five years old and had known Abbas al-Zayyat well.

"A decent man. Never mixed with anyone besides the al-Sadr family and Taha Fawzi, who translated from the Spanish. Or perhaps it was German . . ." He knew nothing about Abbas's daughters: "They were properly raised. Nobody here knew them, not even their names." He told me that Madame al-Nahhas had been their friend. Madame al-Nahhas was the longest-standing resident on the street, and older even than him; her children had all emigrated and she lived alone.

So that same summer, I went to the villa where Madame al-Nahhas lived on the ground floor. At about ten in the morning I pressed the bell by her door. A woman descending the main staircase on her way out of the building said, "She takes a nap after breakfast. Come back in the afternoon and she'll be ready for you." I was impressed that Madame al-Nahhas's schedule was common knowledge on the upper floors. To pass the time, I went on a wander which ended at a Café Cilantro in Mesaha Square, and as I drank my coffee I thought what a fool I'd been. How could I, a perfect stranger, just show up at Madame al-Nahhas's door without calling ahead? How did I think I was going to justify asking all these questions about Enayat? By what right, when I wasn't even a relative? It briefly occurred to me to pass myself off as Enayat's niece, some version of Iman al-Sadr, but I felt that the woman hardly deserved having a trick like that played on her, particularly if she was going to invite me into her home.

So I called Mohammed Samaka, who said he was at work, but could meet me following the afternoon prayers and introduce us. I'll go home, I told myself, and come back later. But there would be no meeting that day. I would have to wait until January 2017 for Madame al-Nahhas to open her door to me.

Her first name was Misyar, she was born in 1938, and she was no relation to al-Nahhas Pasha, though in her living room there was a large photograph showing him witnessing her wedding in 1957.

Once Mohammed Samaka had left us, Misyar asked quite straightforwardly if I would make the tea. I stood in the unfamiliar kitchen taking instructions from next door, until at last I found myself returning with two full mugs and sitting down to face her. She had lived here ever since she got married, she said. Her daughter wanted her to come and live with them in

Seattle but she only felt comfortable here. My eyes fastened on the intricate lace of the curtains and she said that her mother had cut those curtains, which is why she had never changed them, even though they let the light in. Then she was talking about her mother's taste, how she'd never known anything like it; about her astonishment, when she visited her daughter in America, to find her so besotted with modern furniture.

The al-Zayyats had come to the street the year she'd got married, but she only got to know them after she met Enayat, only a year and a half or so before her death.

Then Misyar fell silent, as though she had forgotten I was there. How had she met Enayat?

"I had a cousin, who'd been doing a PhD in literature in Austria. He returned to Egypt around the time I was due to give birth to my daughter, or immediately afterwards, at least, because there's a photograph of him celebrating the Sebou with us seven days later. Anyway, he came back in 1961, and was meant to take up a post in the Foreign Ministry, but he had to wait for security clearance for about a year, so while he was waiting he got a job as a translator at the German Archaeological Institute in Zamalek. He was about six years older than me; I was closer to his younger sister."

Misyar started talking about her aunt, Saad's mother, and her house in Hadayiq al-Qubba, converted to a school after nationalization, and about all her sons and daughters, Misyar's cousins. The stories were entertaining enough, but I was worried she'd forget the question and our time would run out. I had to make a conscious effort not to rush her. But she didn't forget and without prompting returned to Enayat.

"My cousin Saad was madly in love with Enayat."

Love. Why had it never occurred to me? It was shocking to think that I had taken everything Nadia and Azima had told me at face value, had made a point of looking for any gaps in the stories they told—the family, school, friendship, marriage, divorce, the court case, motherhood, writing, publication, depression, suicide—and yet had treated a twenty-four-year-old Enayat, full of life and femininity, and to all intents and purposes divorced since March 1961 when the senior members of both families had met together to persuade Kamal Eddin Shaheen to follow the Book's injunction to *part from them honorably*—I had treated this Enayat as though she were incapable of loving or being loved. I remembered Hosn Shah's line—*a happy woman cannot kill herself over a book*—and it felt to me as though Enayat's life was too much for me to ever know, and yet . . . and yet the line demanded to be played with. *A happy woman cannot kill herself over a court case*, say, or *over a custody battle*, or *for love*. In point of fact, there's nothing to prevent a woman committing suicide for any of these reasons or none at all. But what does it mean, *a happy woman*?

Misyar met Enayat at the Gezira Club. She was there with Saad and his younger sister. Pure chance. They would laugh together at all the coincidences: "I used to live next to her in Mounira, and my school, the Lycée, was in Bab al-Louq like hers, then we moved to the same street in Dokki—but we had to wait until Saad came back from Austria before we met."

Their friendship really took hold in Enayat's final year, even after Saad married his cousin Madiha a fortnight before he was due to travel to Bern to become cultural attaché at the Egyptian

Embassy. This was three or four months before Enayat died. Misyar was the closest person to Enayat at this time.

What was the last time she had seen her?

"My daughter was ill, and Enayat came over to see how she was doing. She didn't come in, we just chatted at the door. I was surprised that she wasn't already up in Alexandria with Nadia as she'd planned. She was very calm, and it was like she'd just come back from the hairdresser's, only her hair was in this really short, peculiar cut. I told her to come in, but she said she had an appointment and would stop by tomorrow. Only the next day she didn't come, and then the day after that I heard the news."

I wanted to ask her about Enayat's relationship with Nadia Lutfi during this period, but she had moved on to Saad, who'd had serious problems with his father and Gamal Abdel Nasser. A few years later he had left the Foreign Ministry to take up a post at a university somewhere in America, then moved to a Canadian university. He had died about ten years ago, maybe more.

Enayat had been writing her second novel, Misyar casually declared to my astonishment. She'd lost all hope of having the first one published and she was getting into her second.

Did Misyar know what it was about?

"About the life of a German botanist who lived in Egypt. Saad read some of it and said that she should forget the first book—the one she couldn't get published—and finish this one. She agreed."

I probed further, but couldn't seem to make the connections. Who was this German botanist? And what was his relationship with the German Archaeological Institute in the novel? My conversation with Madame al-Nahhas sent me back to Enayat's papers, to the two pages I had failed to understand, and then to translate Isolde Lehnert's article on Ludwig Keimer, on the basis that he was the man about whom Enayat had meant to write.

I finally left Madame al-Nahhas at half past seven, with her promise to show me the picture of her with Saad and Enayat, then more of Saad at his wedding, and of Saad's daughter, Sharifa, who was now a famous lawyer in Canada.

I was welcome to come again.

On November 12, 2018, I went back to Sherbiny Street. As I came to Astra Square, I looked around for Mohammed Samaka and saw Ghannam instead, sunning himself in the same spot he'd been sitting the last time I came. I greeted him and said that I would drop in on Madame al-Nahhas then come to see him.

"I'll be waiting."

"Have you seen Mohammed Samaka today?" I asked. "I'd like to say hello."

"God help him, he doesn't get out any more. He was crossing the Corniche in Maadi on his way to see a friend in hospital and a car ran into him. Thank God he survived, for the kids' sake."

Misyar was in a wretched state: a bad cold and coughing horribly. Seemed suddenly aged. I didn't stay long. Could I make her anything to drink? Mint, please, but she didn't tell me where it was, as though this was my home, not hers. By a miracle I found it. Not much later, I was getting up to leave.

I'd be back in Egypt in February, I told her, and I'd see her then, but I sensed I might not and felt sorry for her.

On a chair outside the paint shop, I sat alongside Ghannam al-Magedy and gazed up at Enayat's old balcony. There were no washing lines out, nothing to suggest the inhabitants were home.

I climbed the stairs. The apartment doors on the upper floors dated from the seventies and eighties (a reflection of their then owners' tastes, with one a grim slab of sheet metal) but the first- and second-floor apartments retained their fifties originals, as though the same carpenter had made them as a pair. I took a photograph of the front door to Enayat's apartment: a heavy wooden frame, with the door itself divided into two panels, the upper half holding two panes of frosted glass behind a fret of ironwork lotuses. This was the door that led to her solitude, to her writing and the long nights. I reached out and touched the wood. Would an expert still be able to identify her fingerprints after all these years? I couldn't say, but somehow I was sure that she was in there. When I heard feet climbing the stairs, I panicked. Then grinned: two teenagers, carrying a bike upstairs.

I went downstairs, and out.

Enayat used to dream of leaving this building and this street behind:

I want my feet to feel new ground beneath them, away from this building and the street that leads here, and to know new people too, and a way of thinking that lends life new flavor. Dear tomorrow, give me a magic carpet to fly to other worlds, for I'm in love with the unknown.

But it wasn't possible to abscond with Saad or travel on her own: she was a mother and she couldn't leave her only child behind. She walked this street for the very last time on the evening of January 3, 1963. Hair clipped short, she'd stopped by to see Madame al-Nahhas, and then, perhaps, had kept that mysterious appointment she'd spoken of. But in any case, as she'd climbed the stairs to her apartment, she had known that the only unknown, for her, was death.

When I saw Misyar again in February 2019, her health was restored and she was in a buoyant mood. Her daughter had come over for the Christmas holidays and they had gone together to see her younger sister in Alexandria.

"She's aged a bit, you see. She can't come down to Cairo."

I asked how old she was.

"Four years younger than me," she said, and cackled.

Her daughter had gone through the apartment and now Misyar knew where the pictures were, the ones she had talked about last time. She took up her stick and walked across to a cherrywood cabinet, the top half of which was entirely made of glass, like something you might find in the reading room of a venerable university. I got up to help. Shifting the stick to her left hand she swung back the door on the lower half and I could see a shelf inside, the width of the cabinet. She gestured—"Fetch that album, there"—so I picked it out and we sat down side by side on the sofa. Setting the stick down, she opened the album.

Misyar: very young and very pretty. There was a faint tremor in her hand which hadn't been there before. She was determined to introduce me to everyone in every photograph, and tell me what had become of them. If I hadn't known there was a portrait of Enayat somewhere among them, I could happily have spent the day asking her about these faces.

Enayat sits on the very sofa I am sitting on, but the fabric that covers it is unpatterned. Her hair reaches down to her shoulders and the neck of her dress (or blouse?) is cut low. No earrings, the neck bare, her wide eyes half smiling and her lips clamped shut. An expression like anticipation or uncertainty, as though it shows an instant clipped from a moment of fateful importance. Next to her, Misyar is posing with her daughter on her knees; the little girl confronts the camera decisively and elegantly. In the background, a handsome young man leans forward into the frame, his hands spread wide on the back of the sofa, but touching neither of the women. He wears a black suit jacket over a shirt and is tieless. What can be seen of his trousers is either grey or a light blue. This must be 1962.

Did she remember the picture being taken?

"My husband took it. It was March, his birthday. Saad knew he'd be going to Berlin in September, to work in our embassy, and he was taking training courses at the Ministry of Foreign Affairs."

As for Nadia and Enayat's relationship: "Nadia was busy with the films, unfortunately, and it affected Enayat a great deal because Nadia was the closest person to her. That's what she said to me . . ." I waited for her to go on. I'd no idea which question to ask out of the whirlwind that had filled my head. Then, suddenly:

"Such a pity! Enayat had a custody case over her son. She couldn't marry or leave the country . . .

"A couple of weeks before he traveled, Saad married Madiha, from his father's side of the family . . .

"I never knew how in love with him Enayat was. She wasn't the kind to talk. But Saad was madly in love with her. He came round to see me the day before he left, but wasn't able to see her . . .

"She'd lost hope of publishing her first book, and she was enjoying her work at the German Institute. She was writing another novel about a man called Kameer. . . '

And I said:

"It's Keimer. Ludwig Keimer."

20.

On April 21, 1967, *al-Musawwar* ran a short piece by Mahmoud Amin al-Alem entitled "She Died Even as She Triumphed."

Al-Alem opens: *Literary expression, for the woman, is the most sophisticated of the battles she wages for freedom—freedom in love, freedom to work, freedom of thought, freedom to engage and participate; her freedom as a female, as a mother, and as a human being.*

It is the restrictions faced by women, both visible and invisible, that in his opinion make their literature such a passionate call for freedom: *Shahrazad saved herself from the brute cruelty of Shahriyar by controlling him with help from the diverting tales in which she hides herself. But the new Shahrazad saves herself from a Shahriyar who is society as a whole, and not with stories, but with positive self-expression: labor and struggle and thought and literature.*

He lays out his ideology, his faith in literature's capacity to change society. To al-Alem, literature operates like any form of intellectual engagement or social and political struggle: it plays a role in the creation of our *new, human lives.*

After this brief introduction, he gets to the point:

I am here to tell the story of an author, whose story is the tragedy of our contemporary literature. She is Enayat al-Zayyat, and just weeks ago her novel, Love and Silence, *was published. She never got to see it, because she departed this life before this book was ever released into it. A novel that was a summation of her life, and at the same time, a terrible end to that life. Years ago, she submitted the manuscript to a publisher. When it was rejected she felt that her entire existence had been rejected with it. So she took sleeping pills and slept forever. An act that, strange to say, completely contradicted the spirit of her novel.*

He wonders if Enayat's suicide was a reaction to the failure of her literary philosophy, or perhaps a renunciation of the struggle for freedom. In which respect—at least in my opinion—al-Alem might have been the only person to have posed a serious and sincere question about Enayat's death. He uncouples it from abstract expressions of sympathy, or blanket blame of the publisher that turned her down, or the desire to instrumentalize it in the pursuit of some cause, though all these things might be perfectly legitimate. Instead he points to shortcomings in the very concept of individual freedom:

Freedom cannot be reached by the self alone; it needs others. And when these others turn away from us, then our freedom is rendered barren. It becomes a loss and a tragedy. I do not excuse her suicide but rather explain it. She was young, not yet experienced enough to expand her vision of freedom, to see further than the obstacles which she had encountered piecemeal during her struggle for freedom. She had no comrades to accompany her down this rocky road, and she was of course an artist, a deeply sensitive person.

One might think that *comrades* might be in reference to a social or political movement, a collective vision that creates a wider context in which individual freedom might come about. This version of individualism, which requires the collective to expand the scope of freedoms and assist the individual over the obstacles they face, is in complete accord with al-Alem's idea that the ultimate purpose in all this is the creation of a *new, human life.*

Latifa al-Zayyat started from a similar belief in the importance of the collective to the individual, but she chose to concentrate on isolation as the inescapable, existential condition of Enayat's life. In "She Died and Died Not," a tiny article less than three hundred words long, published in *al-Hiwar* magazine on December 2, 1967, Latifa talked about silence as death's twin:

Silence is a stone, locked down without windows or doors, its still air stirred to a storm by the cry for help which catches in our throats, by the response to that cry which catches in the throats of our loved ones, by words half-heard, half-made, dismembered, incomplete and formless, by the cries of wounded animals, dying in their lairs and burrows, cries that no one hears, or would understand if they did.

Latifa is talking about Enayat, who died in—and by—this silence when she was twenty-five years old, but she also talks about the living, herself included: *The words catch in our throats and we are silent. Alive in our burrows, dying.*

Al-Alem and Latifa al-Zayyat both belong to the generation that immediately preceded Enayat's (al-Alem was born in 1922, Latifa a year later) and since the 1940s both had been steeped in the same attitudes to political consciousness and activism. Both lived as part of a group or collective of some kind, real or theoretical, for all that they might have doubted in its existence during those periods of self-imposed silence, or prison, or exile. Enayat was not afforded this opportunity. In life and death alike she remained on the margins, a writer outside the milieu of cultural exchange, without mentors or foremothers or contemporaries. Even now, fifty years after the publication of her first novel, it is difficult to assign her to any group or movement.

So Latifa al-Zayyat differs from al-Alem in trying to imagine Enayat's silence and inner isolation. It is not only her gender that allows her to do this, but the fact of her own personal journey, which followed a long silence she wrote about in *The Search: Personal Papers.* By 1946, Latifa was a leading figure in the labor and student movements, and alongside her first husband was being pursued by the security forces in the form of the political police, but in 1952 she abandoned collective activism and married an ideological enemy, Rashad Rushdi. Why? *He was the first man to wake the woman in me,* she wrote. What happened next she would describe as paralysis, as being trapped in her error, as having her own blood on her hands, yet even so she continued to pursue her own personal projects: love, a doctorate, her novel *The Open Door.* In 1965, she asked for a divorce, and then, just as she was finding her voice again after her long silence, came the 1967 defeat to Israel.

In 1954, al-Alem lost his job as an assistant lecturer in philosophy at Cairo University, along with his leftist and communist colleagues, and went to work for the *Roz al-Youssef* magazine. He played a vital part in coordinating the many different communist organizations and the formation of the Egyptian Communist Party in 1955. His "movement name" was Farid, under which moniker he issued a communiqué from the party's political bureau supporting the union of Egypt and Syria in 1958, but criticizing its implementation for failing to respect the distinct characteristics of both peoples. On New Year's Eve, 1959, he was arrested and spent the next five years (plus a few months) in prison.

According to his own account, the day after his release, he was contacted by a friend who was then working at Sami Sharaf's office, saying that he was to take him to meet Sharaf, and at this meeting Sharaf asked him to consider joining the state-approved Vanguard Organization. He agreed. He was given an office at the Revolutionary Leadership Council, and when he proposed issuing a cultural publication, he was placed in charge of both the magazine and cultural affairs at the organization. Then came the defeat of 1967.

I had some idea that the four-year delay between Enayat's suicide and the publication of her novel must have been connected in some way with the structural changes that were taking place in 1963 within government-run publishing institutions. Tharwat Okasha has written that *in 1963, al-Qawmiyya Publishing was merged with a new institution called the Institute for News and Publishing*, and that its attempt to live up to its slogan—*a book every six hours*—led to failure as a commercial enterprise. When Okasha was reappointed Minister of Culture in 1966, he merged all ministry-controlled publishing imprints into a single printing and publishing company which he named Arab Writer Publishing, placing it under Mahmoud Amin al-Alem's direction.

My guess was that the man who implemented the annual schedule at Arab Writer Publishing was the man who ushered Enayat's novel into the light. But Niam al-Baz, a journalist who had been born in 1935, just a year before Enayat, told me a quite different story about the novel's journey, one that predates both al-Alem's arrival on the scene and its author's self-isolation:

"I was very good friends with Adel al-Ghadban. He was a great cultural figure, and single-handedly kept Dar al-Maaref going. He gave me three or four of Enayat's stories to look at and I really liked them, so I asked if I could meet her. He told me she was the daughter of a friend of his, and she was trying to get the stories published, but not under her real name. I found that so strange. At the time, I was working for *al-Jeel*, and there weren't many girls writing back then; I couldn't believe I'd found one and might get to be her friend. I begged Adel to put me in touch, and he disappears for a week then hands me her number. I called her and she said she couldn't meet me. I kept pushing—I'm a journalist and I'm pushy, there's no such thing as impossible—and went to meet her at her home in Heliopolis. Still married, at home with the baby.

"This incredibly beautiful woman, in a palatial apartment looking out over the Merryland Gardens. She didn't really get me at first, my way of speaking. I started to choose my words more carefully when she didn't laugh at any of my stories. It was embarrassing. I asked her why she didn't want her name to appear on the stories, and she was very reserved.

'It's a private matter,' she said. I got the feeling she wasn't the type who cared to get to know me, and she didn't want me knowing her, either.

"I never saw her outside. The second time I went to see her, she had moved to Dokki, and it took me aback to find the apartment pretty much empty, even though she was from a rich family. You walked in, and there was this beautiful rug with a couple of chairs standing on it, and a bedroom with a desk. She'd furnished one bedroom for her son and left the other one completely bare. The kitchen had a gas oven and a fridge and things to make tea and coffee, and that was it. When I laughed and asked her what was going on, she told me she'd always dreamed of having an empty apartment just like this, and I waited for her to go on, but that was all she had to say. In Dokki, she talked eagerly about the novel she was writing, but that aside, I got the impression she'd no particular desire to be my friend and no interest in going out and doing things, and I didn't see her again.

"After I'd read the draft of her novel, I phoned her to tell her that she was a great writer, and that I found the way the novel ended with Ahmed's death deeply affecting.

"When we heard the news of her suicide, Adel al-Ghadban was very moved and he tried to get the novel published anywhere he could. Dar al-Maaref had been nation-alized by then, you see, and there was a government appointee in overall command. He tried al-Qawmiyya, but they told him they didn't like the ending, and he said that the author was dead, so she couldn't change it. They didn't like the ending, then: they wanted it to finish on a positive note, and neither Adel nor her father would give their consent, so it all fell through."

This was over a phone call. I hadn't expected Niam al-Baz to spring any surprises on me, but she had done, and without even meaning to. Niam al-Baz was one of a number of Enayat's contemporaries who were subjected to my frequent and unpredictable phone calls. I grew used to the responses:

"No, I've never heard the name."

"We never met, but I've read the novel."

"We never met and I haven't read the novel."

This last was the wholly unexpected answer of one of the most important writers and critics of Enayat's generation, Safinaz Kazem. I'd been so hoping that she had known her.

Fortunately for me, Niam's daughter was in the apartment when I called, because her mother was hard of hearing. She took the call, repeating my questions to Niam, and I would hear Niam give the answers in her clear, powerful voice.

But now I changed tactics, putting the same question to her over and over:

"The novel didn't end with the July Revolution and the column of tanks on parade?"

"You're saying the novel ended with Ahmed's death?"

"The novel's ending was changed at al-Qawmiyya?"

And time after time, Niam al-Baz would give the same answer back: "Yes," "That's right," "I'm sure of it."

Now I had no actual proof that the ending of *Love and Silence* was altered by al-Qawmiyya, but I went back to the edition I had, the text published three months before the defeat of 1967, to look at the ending again. Reading those words on the cover—THE UNITED ARAB REPUBLIC—MINISTRY OF CULTURE—I felt the futility of any attempt to "find the truth." Despite the failure of its union with Syria in 1961, Egypt remained a "United Republic" right up until 1971.

Who cared if some officer had slapped a happy ending on a novel whose author was dead and gone?

As Enayat was ending her life in January 1963, al-Alem and most of his comrades were in Oases Prison, engaging in philosophical debates, writing plays and novels, and planting the desert with vegetables. They were eagerly following the progress of, and cheering on, the very man who had imprisoned them: Gamal Abdel Nasser. Beneath Latifa al-Zayyat's feet, the ground was shaking. Since 1960, she had felt paralyzed, incapable of acting, unable to write a thing; what strength she had, she used to request a divorce and make her return to collectivist action.

Al-Alem and Latifa al-Zayyat reached Enayat down two parallel tracks. In his article from April 1967, he had emphasized the importance of the collective in redeeming the individual and equipping them for a new life; Latifa's piece, published in December 1967, contained no such hope. Between these two articles lies the defeat.

I tried imagining Enayat as a member of the Egyptian Communist Party. Imagined her getting to know al-Alem and other comrades and writing a sincerely positive conclusion to her novel. I imagined the novel being published in 1961. Life going on. In this scenario, though, she would have to free herself from the illusion of her individual freedom; she might have to take a "movement name" chosen by a Party official; perhaps she would go to prison or go on the run. But what guarantee could there be that a woman with Enayat's constitution would be protected from suicide by the collective?

Maybe if she'd been from a politicized family, like Latifa's, or had gone to university before getting married, she would have been able to meet men and women who were like her, would have joined and left their various groups and circles. If she'd been one of those middle-class women writers, attending seminars and literary salons, she would have come across poet Gamila al-Alaily, and they might have discussed May Ziadeh together. After the meeting of the Pan-Arabist poets had finished, Galila Rida would take her out to a café where, of course, she would tell Enayat how she, Galila, had inspired the poet Ibrahim Nagi, and that he wrote a poem about her. Maybe she would read Enayat some of her erotic poems. Better yet, Enayat would visit Galila's apartment in Shubra and meet her son, Galal, who lived with cerebral atrophy after contracting meningitis when he was three. Imagine. If she'd had these opportunities, her idea of what it means to suffer would have been broadened, and Galila, with her strength and love of life, might have become her role model.

It is possible to construct scenarios by the dozen in which Enayat is caught up in the lives of other people and enticed down from her tower to engage with the world. It is easy to imagine her explaining to Niam al-Baz why she did not want her name to go on her short stories, or why, for that matter, she dreamed of an empty apartment—the hole in the wall of cold upper-class decorum picked wider. But this is how Enayat lived and died: part of no scene, literary or social or political, in an Egypt where people were tribes and nations, where there were no individuals but only ideologies in blocs.

But why should she remain a prisoner of the sixties? Didn't she herself say that she'd been born *at the wrong time*, that she dreamed of rubbing herself out and being born again? Let's say instead that Enayat al-Zayyat had been a nineties writer, and I'd run into her by chance in Cairo in 1990. Two young women writers who spoke two different languages, or, say, who spoke no language at all, and had no political project to consume our lives, no collective dream to keep us bright-eyed through the night. There were no literary giants such as Anis Mansour and Youssef al-Sebaie, but neither was there an Oases Prison. A great vacuum that we gladly turned our backs on. I'd found her repressed and fragile and aloof, her class worn as a shield. I don't know how she'd seen me: most likely, she couldn't really see anyone outside herself.

The truth is that friendship between us had been impossible. If it had been me who'd committed suicide, Enayat wouldn't have been sad so much as remorseful because she hadn't tried to know me. But it was Enayat who had killed herself in January 1993, and what I'd felt was grief and guilt in equal measure, because I had believed in her talent and was waiting for her to live a life of writing, because I understood her pain but hadn't known how to tell her.

A powerful desire to treat her cruelly. Maybe the only feeling I hadn't yet had towards Enayat. What if, I asked myself?

Suppose . . .

Suppose Enayat had continued to pursue her writing, and that this had become her purpose, her identity. She had never understood what it meant for the state to engineer cultural projects in the post-revolution era, hadn't known of the celebrity artists and famous political activists inside the prisons and outside, and the less famous too, and the networks that connected them, and the battles in which literature and politics and publishing were one. She simply hadn't known.

What happened to Enayat happens frequently. A writer cut off from their peers is transformed into a tragic figure, their delusions (of persecution, of grandeur, of nihilistic despair) ballooning in this isolation until they finally come to what awaits them: to an appointment in some moribund cultural institution, to mysticism or bitter resentment, to the self-obsession and puritanical righteousness of the self-made, or to open support for a murderous regime. They might go back to their family, though they believed they would never return. They might end up a hero, after all: the hero who refuses all and any of these paths and steps away from their life.

Maybe that's what happened. That Enayat went to war for her individuality and waited for victory in the form of al-Qawmiyya's acceptance: that is, victory granted by the very society against which she fought. Her divorce was a battle won, as was writing a novel and going to work at the German Archaeological Institute. But losing the custody battle was a defeat. The novel's rejection was a defeat. Her best friend's lack of availability was a defeat. Sacrificing love for motherhood was a defeat. Faced with all these defeats, what could the free individual do but take a final leap into the void?

Enayat photographed by Nadia Lutfi in 1961

21.

So I went to the archives at Akhbar al-Yom *and requested their file on Enayat al-Zayyat. The index showed a file registered in her name—No. 42620—but the file itself was missing. Two more days asking questions, then the director told me that about ten years back an expert was brought in to update the archive, and he had told them that any file which hadn't been updated in the last five years wasn't worth keeping. They destroyed them all. Fucking "expert."*

This email was sent to me on March 10, 2015, by my friend Mohamed Shoair, as a summary of his investigations in the archives of the newspaper where he worked.

During my own research, I had encountered archives at any number of magazines and newspapers which contained not a single mention of Enayat. As far as these archives were concerned, she never existed at all: not even as a name and number. Put another way, she is a person that these institutional archives do not see or acknowledge. She had foreseen this herself. In the autumn of 1962, she wrote in her journal:

I don't mean a thing to anybody. Lost, found, it's all the same: here is as good as gone. The world wouldn't tremble either way. When I walk I leave no tracks, like I walk on water, and I am unseen, invisible.

Sometimes, something will turn up in the wrong place, in a file of clippings about Latifa al-Zayyat, for instance, or under Nadia Lutfi's name, either because she had mentioned Enayat's name in an interview or because their names had been mentioned together and the star's had taken precedence. But at *Akhbar al-Yom*, Enayat had both a name and a file number; it was the file itself that was gone. I have no idea what that file contained.

In 2017, I looked through file 8245 at the *Dar al-Hilal* archives, but when I returned in 2019 the employee said, "It's not here. Most likely marked for destruction. Last year, they decided they could do without a lot of our files."

Marked for destruction does not happen by accident or as a result of casual negligence; it is a deliberate action made on the request of the expert who draws a distinction between inactive files—those which take up space without ever being requested or augmented—and active files, which remain open to the future. In other words, the institutional archive, which is created, maintained, and used as a system, can become burdensome, and requires a supplementary system to facilitate its own destruction.

The ideology behind the creation of the archive is the same which takes the decision to destroy it. To the archival specialist, important files are those which are requested by researchers and journalists, or which continue to expand in size over time. Forgotten files are, necessarily, those which deal with marginal events or less important individuals: the things that no one cares about.

The archive is a manifestation of civilization: an embodied desire to preserve the contiguity, plurality, and contradictions that together make up a collective memory. At the same time, it is inevitably a reflection of a culture's awareness of its own memory. During periods of decline, that memory begins to fade, which is when the specialist is brought in to distinguish what is important from what is trivial.

I told Yasser Abdellatif the story of Enayat's file at *Akhbar al-Yom*, and he had an entirely different take on the subject:

"Contempt for historical value isn't just an abstract idea. How do you explain someone pissing against a protected monument when there's all of God's wide world to use? Forget high-flown rhetoric about abdicating your duty to the past and selling out your heritage. Throughout the early 2000s there was this constant financial shortfall at state television, and they never had enough money to buy new tape to record their shows. So how did they solve it? Once an episode had been broadcast—a week later, say—it would be wiped from the tape and a new episode recorded over the top. A new Betacam tape cost about two hundred pounds at the time and they'd wipe an old episode that might have cost tens of thousands to make then record a new one over the top. And there were no back-ups for the old episodes. From 1998 to 2000, the programs being made were possibly the bravest and most experimental in Egyptian television history, and they were all deleted. Nothing survived, not a single episode."

Yasser didn't have a final answer for why this might be so, but he used an expression that stuck with me. He said, "There's something we might term 'the nihilism of the archive,' in the sense Nietzsche meant when he wrote: *the historical moment in which all values are baseless.*"

One particularly prominent feature of the archive's nihilism is that its physical absence—or a lack of interest in revisiting it when it *is* available—is perceived as a license to go on endlessly reproducing the claims of other people, unquestioningly and without substantiation. This is commonly referred to as a culture of uncritical adoption, but I believe any piece of terminology naming this process should include the words "nihilism" or "despair." It is a despair at the value and meaning of research, a despair over the possibility of knowing.

I felt it myself, was overwhelmed by its misery, as I hunted for any trace of Enayat al-Zayyat. In the Ministry of Culture's archives there was nothing on al-Qawmiyya's publication policy, no list of the books that had been submitted and never published, and no record of the reasons for their rejection. Which is perhaps understandable: there is no particular reason why an authoritarian culture ministry should preserve anything at all about a writer who had made no contribution to its project to homogenize and disseminate a "national culture." But my research had failed to turn up even a record of what had been published or any reports from the cultural committees responsible for book publishing and strategy. In the court archives, whole case files had vanished along with any documentary trace of their existence, and it would have been impossible to recover them without bribing court officials to undertake the research, because the indexing system was a hybrid of several different archival systems. Getting what you wanted there was a matter of luck. The national archives held treasures, watched over by a staff who suspected the intentions of each and every researcher that came to them: until you could prove otherwise, research was, by definition, a breach of national security.

It amazed me that something as simple as locating the first edition of a given novel required you to visit the national library, since modern publishing houses don't transcribe all the necessary data in subsequent editions. If you were looking into the evolution of psychiatric medicine in Egypt, say, or the history of the German community and their educational and medical institutions in twentieth-century Cairo, then your only option was to search for books on these subjects in languages other than Arabic.

The absence of Enayat's writings from the canon of the Arabic novel is yet another aspect of this nihilism. In 1999, Bouthaina Shaaban wrote *Voices Revealed: Arab Women Novelists 1898–2000*, in which she protests the marginalization of women writers in Arabic. Yet she makes no mention of *Love and Silence* or its author. You could argue that this isn't so very significant. After all, her book only deals with writing that was successful, that had managed to leap the barrier into the canon: that is to say, those novels which men had already deemed worthy of inclusion. The nihilism here is not her failure to research all novels by women, it is the fact that her omission of so many of these novels was, in fact, necessary. It allowed Bouthaina Shaaban to repeat, without fear of contradiction, what we had read and would continue to read in so many other studies: that Arab women writers were primarily concerned with nationalism, that there could be no liberation for women without the liberation of the nation, that the seminal text in this context was *The Open Door* by Latifa al-Zayyat. These platitudes are repeated so often that when attention does turn to *Love and Silence* it is approached through a frame which has been created in its absence and which obliges the novel to be read against, or alongside, *The Open Door*. Then there is the standard mis-apprehension that the novel was written in 1967 and that the author had killed herself that same year.

Anis Mansour had succeeded in painting a picture of Enayat—the suicide who'd been his dearest friend, whom he'd taken under his wing and whose stories he'd published in *al-Jeel* in 1960, whose novel he even claimed to have pub-lished—and this image of her was embellished and expanded over the next forty years, without any of it leading to the novel itself being read or reissued, or indeed without any serious attempt to test his claims.

But the archive tells us that Anis Mansour never published any of Enayat's stories, not in *al-Jeel* nor anywhere else, not in 1960 and not afterwards. And what of that story he would repeat time and time again, about how he'd recalled a sen-tence from her novel on a trip to Yemen and had recited it to Youssef al-Sebaie, only for al-Sebaie to inform him that its author had died? Its origin can be unearthed by going back to the archive of Mansour himself.

On July 23, 1963—that is, roughly six months after Enayat's death—Anis Mansour wrote a piece in *al-Musawwar* entitled "The Unknown Author Died." It opens with a long scene, played for laughs, about the time he shared a cabin with Youssef al-Sebaie as part of a delegation of writers traveling to Yemen: the heat, the humidity, his insomniac envy of al-Sebaie's ability to sleep like a baby through it all.

Then he writes the following:

And suddenly, Youssef al-Sebaie sat down, and asked me, "Do you know so-and-so?" and I responded, not very encouragingly, by asking him why he wanted to know. What did the heat and discomfort of our present situation have to do with that girl? While he was considering his answer, I stared at him, feeling as though we were characters in No Exit, *the play by the existentialist philosopher Sartre; that we were both naked, and in hell; that we were dead now, and that there was no need to lie any more, for the dead cannot lie . . .*

"Yes," I said, "I know her."

"Did you like her stories?"

"She approached me a few months ago and mentioned your name. She said she'd shown you her novel. What did you think of her writing?"

And he said: "The truth is I liked it very much indeed, and I told her straight out that I would be prepared to publish it and to help her in any way I could, because she was talented. I actually sent her along to the state publishers, but I don't know what happened exactly."

Youssef al-Sebaie fell silent for a moment, then went on:

"It was strange, though. She had no self-confidence. She didn't believe she was a talented writer."

I tore off half my clothes and perched Gandhi-like on the edge of the bunk. This conversation, I felt, was like the goat that Gandhi

*had taken with him everywhere he went: to go on talking would be
like wringing milk from that bony creature's udders.*

I said:

*"She really is talented. A few years ago, I read a number of her
stories and published one of them under her name, and another one
under an assumed name. She was delighted. When I get back to
Cairo I must try and get in touch with her again, because I've promised to write an introduction to a collection of her short stories . . ."*

Mansour tells al-Sebaie (and the reader) about the unexpected phrasing the young woman uses, and puts it down
to her not being influenced by Egyptian writers. He asks
al-Sebaie to publish her in *Roz al-Youssef* and says that he will
publish her in *al-Jeel*. But then al-Sebaie tells him what has
happened: *"Allah!" he blurted. "You didn't know? She's dead."*

In 1963, Mansour makes no mention of the name of this
unknown author; she is nameless. Nor does he say anything
about her novel or why it should be published. He is sad-
dened when al-Sebaie tells him of her death, although just
minutes before he had been reluctant to talk about her, and
had waited to hear what al-Sebaie had to say before venturing
his own opinion.

*I felt the cabin had grown hotter, that the sweat was flowing
freer, the tiny beads turning to fat drops and each drop scalding me,
as though some chemical process had transformed the perspiration
which covered my naked flesh into tears. I felt that our conversation
must pause, out of respect, at this poor, talented girl, who had
so suddenly and secretly appeared, who had no belief in her own
talent, and nor, it seemed, did anyone else. But she had persisted,
determined to be a hero in a story without clear principles, its author*

unknown, a story that no one read or cared to read, save two or three people who then became temporarily distracted by their own quotidian problems and cares. But she hastened the ending: she cut her story short and deprived her readers.

In this narrative, Mansour and al-Sebaie are a pair of high priests presiding over the worlds of literature, culture, and publishing, yet they have divided the task between them: one has promised her an introduction to her short stories and will publish her in *al-Jeel*, and the other has sent her novel to the state publishers and will publish her in *Roz al-Youssef*. "High priest" is the phrase I'd been searching for since I had first encountered Mansour's articles about Enayat. They are always talented, these priests, and powerful. They regard themselves as the arbiters of what might pass for culture. They are always willing to support new talent. But alas, they are also terribly busy.

The reader of this piece might reasonably expect Mansour to have included one of the stories that Enayat gave him, at least to prove his assertions that she was talented and that she used unaffected phrasing, as he'd claimed. But who's to say that this was his goal when writing the piece? The author *deprived her readers*, he says, and in his own way he is doing the same, by augmenting the archive not with the writing of the *unknown author*, but with a story about her. And we must remember: this is his archive and he is the man who knows what others do not, who knows about Sartre's plays and Gandhi's goat.

Mansour does not trouble himself to actually publish Enayat's short stories, but rather retells three of them in his own language. Stranger still, all three have titles, even as the author herself remains nameless: "They Were Here," "A Drop of Water," and "Nothing Happened." Where are these stories? If we are to believe Mansour, they were in his possession but he did not publish them: he saw no reason to add them to the archive of Egyptian short stories nor to couple them to their author's name. If he is lying, and he had only heard of them— or had fabricated them entirely, just as he was subsequently to fabricate his friendship with their author—then that would be an instance of what is known as "falsifying the archive."

So what becomes of the personal archive after the death of the owner, the person who has gathered together its assemblage of stories and journals and letters and notes and drafts? Could it, too, become the burden of those that inherit it, taking up space and appropriating memories? By what ways and means might it be destroyed? What takes its place once it has been disposed of? Can the causes and methods of its destruction be used to help reconstruct it, or reimagine its contents?

Here, we must picture the family extending its authority over one of its members after their death: the cultured, conservative, bourgeois family; the ideological family; the fragmented family. The first of these burns the archive, and this is what happened to Enayat's archive, including the draft of her second novel; all that was left were a few context-less passages from her journal and letters, free-floating and abstractly existential, nothing to trouble the reputation of an established, traditional family. Her father gave permission for some of them to be published in *al-Musawwar* in 1967, and

Nadia Lutfi allowed others to be appended to her interview with Foumil Labib the same year. And then both her sister and Nadia permitted me to take these same pages to use, as though they had become official documents, certified by the passage of time.

The few pages that survived were just the punctuation from the full text of her life. Enayat's anger at her inability to walk in step with the world around her had been effaced, and all that remained was the demure tale that her survivors wanted to see. The life story of a person who committed suicide more than fifty years ago has been reinterpreted, and this interpretation has become the real story. They are not lying when they hide what they know; what they know is painful and must be put away.

The ideological family also exerts its authority over the archive. The religious intellectual, say, will excise sex and modify anti-religious sentiments and phrasing in his parent's archive while the pious publisher colludes with him. The university professor rationalizes her politician father's archive to correlate with her own political beliefs, allowing certain documents to appear at certain times and consigning others to oblivion.

One's best chance, then, lies in the third type: the fragmented family, the family without an image or cause to fight for. Such a family might sell the deceased's papers and books to a bookseller and if the buyer is clever, they might sell them on to the national archives of some up-and-coming Arab state or foreign research institute where they can be easily located and accessed.

Maybe the only real solution here lies in our own, personal interaction with the archive, our willingness as individuals to volunteer our time to discover it and protect it both from institutional destruction and the equally lethal "wishes of the family." The institution has no idea of the value of what it owns, of the papers that lie silent in its files. But what if it found out? Then the hierarchy of intellectual value which it embodies would allow it to destroy anything that does not closely align with its own project. The institution itself is not obliged to define what is and isn't important; quite simply, it does not adopt our questions as its own. Likewise, the family is not where we would turn to understand how one of its members perceives their own life.

Nadia told me so much. Enayat's story is always entwined with her own. Constant proofs were offered of their friendship. She gave me what she was able to give me: photographs of them together, what Enayat had written to her and what she had said about Enayat after her death, and then the few pages she had from Enayat's journal.

But where were Enayat's drawings? Where was the box next to the bed in the spare bedroom? Most likely in the hands of Nadia's son and her assistant Reda, or captive to Nadia's own hesitancy. I have to accept the existence of an authority which protects Nadia from the intrusions of strangers like myself, but must I accept the portrait I have been given of an unwavering friendship? Nadia Lutfi, wife and mother and daughter of a conservative family, who entered the world of cinema in 1958: this was a journey that required adjustments, a negotiation with everyone and everything to achieve the dream. Her re-creation as a star of Egyptian cinema didn't just require her to hit her marks and learn her lines. She had to take on a new name, adopt a new family history, leave a son to be raised by his grandmother, then allow her marriage to collapse. The three years that preceded Enayat's suicide were years of sleeplessness and effort and transformation for the young actress. In those three years alone, she shot seventeen films.

The truth is that Nadia knew nothing of Enayat's love affair, nor did she remember hearing anything about a second novel.

In the memories of those closest to her, Enayat's archive has not been interpreted or treated with any kind of systematic rigor. They have had no experts to advise them, as *Akhbar al-Yom* had. Their approach was dictated by the need of those who loved her to be able to live with their pain. For more than fifty years they had sought to come to terms with the guilt they felt towards this sister, this friend, who had taken her life. What they gave me was the narrative which had been authored in memory after this reconciliation had taken place.

I cannot decide if it is ethical to claim that the traces of all these things—the family, Enayat's relationship with her mother, her friendship with Nadia Lutfi—should have to be reconstituted and placed into her story. It isn't any special respect for privacy or ethical consideration which leads me to avoid this kind of narrative, but rather the fact that following the traces left by a person is not at all the same as telling the story of that person's life. To trace someone does not mean filling all the gaps or searching out every fact in the quest to document it. It is to take a journey towards someone who cannot speak for themselves. It is a dialogue that is perforce one-sided.

The skilful biographer chooses their subject carefully. Conventionally, they start with birth and end at death, filling in the details of the life that runs between the two, researching as much of it as is possible and occasionally fictionalizing. They know what they are going to write about and where they will find their material, and they know the significance of their project to the reader. In truth, they know the reader.

The biographer writes about three types of personality. There is the leader, who has the authority and the abilities to lead others, a category which covers founding fathers of all stripes, be they politicians or military commanders or leaders of social movements. Then there are those who author some innovative or transformative creative act, writers and artists and philosophers and musicians, where the biographer's focus is on the creative process itself: how it came about, what makes it different, why it is so influential. The third type we might term the spiritual personality, whose significance is not measured by material achievement but by their ability to effect real change in the world, to make us aware of its corruption or to allow us to make peace with it.

Which of these was Enayat, I wondered, and was fairly sure that the answer was none of them. Which may be why the institutional archive was unaware of her existence, or was only temporarily aware of her during that brief period in

1967 when her novel was published and her name was heard, only to ignore her again thereafter. Maybe it was the reason I began to follow her, as though her place in the shadows, on the margins of the archive, mirrored Najla's quest for personal freedom in *Love and Silence*, or Enayat's exclusion from the literary and political scene, or even to her suicide. To trace a person that the institutional archive does not acknowledge or permit to remain among its important files means entering the personal archive and its shadow maze: unlit, unforthcoming, and complex.

Sometimes the tracer and the archival researcher have similar experiences. Both encounter irreconcilable and arbitrary facts that need to be contemplated and their connections teased out; both are looking for something credible on which to hang their interpretation. Before Enayat had undergone her transformation from an unknown writer to my siren, before I had ever seen a picture of her or heard a thing about her or felt this strange compulsion to know her—before all that, I was looking for treasure, for the personal archive I knew must be there somewhere, divided between apartments, strewn across Cairo's topography and the memories of those who remained.

At first blush, the destruction of Enayat's archive felt like a catastrophe, but its absence sent me after the traces of its erasure and showed me that my true ambition was not to see her life laid out in the pages of a book. In describing the life of someone who has died we inevitably become complicit in the flattening of the past, the hollowing out of meaning and complexity. I mustn't speak in her name, I told myself; I mustn't present some sketch version of her life. There is a moment of intersection between us and I will use this moment as a spiritual guide; in every other regard we shall be different. Maybe she only exists in the margins where she is spared the authoritarian interventions of institution and family and friends. Should I have followed her traces elsewhere? In what was destroyed, in the geography where she lived and died (the street, the tomb, the German School, the German Institute), in the personal status law and the divorce case, in the contexts in which her novel was rejected and then published, in dreams and friendships and love and depression and death? The stories of all the people whose lives intersected with hers seemed part of her story too. I wanted to get to know them, one by one, because they had passed through her life.

In *Subject to Biography: Psychoanalysis, Feminism, and Writing Women's Lives*, Elisabeth Young-Bruehl reviews what she has learned from writing the biographies of Hannah Arendt and Anna Freud. As I read, I felt the double rush of alarm and joy. Young-Bruehl says what I cannot: that narrating someone else's life is dependent on *feeling the desires of that other person as a means for comparison*. More precisely, it is dependent on the biographer's awareness of the role the subject plays in the biographer's own psychology:

The usual—indeed, the clichéd—way of describing empathy as "putting yourself in another's place" seems to me quite wrong. Empathizing involves, rather, putting another in yourself, *becoming another person's habitat, as it were, but without dissolving the person, without digesting the person. You are mentally pregnant, not with a potential life but with a person; indeed, with a whole life—a person with her history. So the subject lives on in you, and you can, as it were, hear her in this intimacy. But this, as I said, depends on your ability to tell the difference between the subject and yourself, which means to appreciate the role that she plays in your psychic life. Such insight is the ground on which you can distinguish between what you want for yourself, which you may be seeking partly from her, and what she wanted for herself, which she obviously did not seek from you (although you may supply part of what she wanted in the biography).*

22.

Good evening my dear ones, greetings one and all, and welcome back to my study, my port in a storm. I hope all is well
with you and I hope, too, that you'll accept my apologies for
abandoning you out here in such strange circumstances, lumped
together and left alone. Forgive me. You can be exhausting,
you know. Of course I bear some of the responsibility: I failed
to make sense of your fixations, of the things you did and the
things that happened to you. I resorted to laying you out in
order of your dates of death, like a gravedigger.

    Leaner volumes are left breathless beneath the weight of
big fat books, well-bred girls are unnerved by the proximity
of the brash and vulgar, and serious-minded revolutionaries
turn their noses up at the reckless. The more uncompro-
mising feminists loathe everybody. Many of you have never
met your neighbors here, or worse: you might find yourself
lying against, or under, someone who resents or envies you.
Though you're luckier than some: this heater spares you
the horrors of the cold outside. Thank the woman who
owned the place before me, a painter whose studio became

my sanctuary. You are currently ranged along the length of her old work table, now my desk: three meters long and big enough to hold you all.

Seven clipped strides from the back door of my house to the study: the stale air butts my nose, turns to mucus in my lungs. It is two in the morning and over my pajamas I have thrown on a Canada Goose jacket, boots, gloves, and woolly hat, just to see how you were getting on.

OK. That might be overstating it slightly, but you were all on my mind. Your words were bouncing around my brain. Sure, I also wanted a cigarette, but that wouldn't have been enough on its own to get me out here. I remembered that it was January 3, you see. How could I not be with you? And in the spirit of full disclosure: I'm a little unsteady on my feet, under the influence of what the more virtuous among you have never touched.

Let's begin. Here's Aisha al-Taymuriyya, our Turkish-Kurdish-Circassian foremother, whom we celebrate at all our gatherings. Daughter of the writer Ismail Pasha Taymur, she was born in 1840, just as four European nations were busy clipping Mohammed Ali's wings. Cutting the founder of the modern Egyptian state down to size. Some of us might know her from that ridiculous poem she wrote:

> With chaste hand I uphold my hijab's honor
> By modesty held up above my peers
> I make my mirror from the notebook's cover
> My makeup is the inkstain as it smears

Apologies, Aisha. Patience, and you'll see what I'm getting at. As I was saying, our honored foremother wrote truly absurd verse—praise poetry and hymns to the virtues—but she also wrote beautiful poems about nature, including these lines written in Farsi, which I have read in Hussein Mujib al-Masry's Arabic translation:

Bright moon, my bouquet of roses came apart though they were in your care. Who strewed and scattered them? To see my bouquet disarrayed, I feel within myself a grief so strong—such agonies!

And there is this, from the notebook where she recorded her experiences of divine intoxication:

> *What do my critics know*
> *Of what my soul would drink*
> *And what intoxications would receive?*
>
> *Between their dark suspicions and my conscience*
> *Lies a gulf. God knows*
> *My true intentions.*

But then the disaster. Is it the case that all great writing must be born out of catastrophe? Her only daughter, Tawhida, died just days before her wedding, and it was then that Aisha began to write her greatest poetry, entering into a richly productive dialogue with the Arabic elegiac tradition from the time of the Jahiliyya, particularly the poems of al-Khansa. Yet for all that, her name is never mentioned alongside that of Mahmoud Sami al-Baroudi, the supposed pioneer of the revivalist school in modern Arabic poetry, who was a year her junior.

I haven't staggered out here in the small hours simply to defend Aisha al-Taymuriyya, or anyone else for that matter. It's just that I was reading some of what Mervat Hatem wrote about Aisha, and it staggered me how little I knew about her, the sheer range of her cosmopolitanism, the contradictions and frustrations she felt as a woman living in the nineteenth century. That in 1887 she had called for women to be educated and had championed the need for female literacy, for instance, but at the same time had also attacked the progressive champion Qasim Amin for being westernized, and then towards the end of her life had burned many of her poems.

Here you lie, generation on generation, ranged before me. Aisha on her own at one end of the table, then a group of writers with flowers as pseudonyms, followed by the writers of the Arab Enlightenment. These last were often aristocrats, their fathers and brothers and husbands prominent intellectuals of the late nineteenth and early twentieth centuries. And something else that I hadn't noticed before: most were incomers and immigrants, Beirut to Alexandria, Damascus to Brazil, Ashmit to Louisiana.

To summarize our progress: more than twenty published novels written by women prior to 1904.

Back to it. Here is May Ziadeh, and alongside May a group of her contemporaries, then another group who came to prominence during the revolution of 1919. From the early 1950s there's a set of westernized Levantines and Egyptians who alarmed everyone with their titles (*The Ungovernable Girl, The Restless Night, The Carnal Curse, I Am Alive, Memoirs of a Mannish Woman, The Night and I, Just One Night*) until we come to the 1960s and the two al-Zayyats with their two different yet complementary approaches to writing about the world. One we all read and were influenced by; the other was set aside.

But we are talking about writing in the broadest sense, broader than poetry and the novel. So next to the al-Zayyats let us have Inji Aflatoun and all those writers who were denied entry to the gated garden of High Literature. Doriya Shafik is one of these women. In 1940 she returned with her doctorate from Paris, convinced that she was going to change the status of women in Egypt. Aisha Abd al-Rahman was another: she had been writing, and being published, since the early 1930s, when she was just eighteen years old. And then there's Safinaz Kazem, still writing to this day. I recommend you read her piece in *al-Jeel* from 1959 about her adventures in Europe.

Of course that's not the end of the story. This table can only hold Enayat's contemporaries and predecessors. But please don't get me wrong: I'm not here to prove that Arab women writers exist, or to argue that *good* Arab women writers exist. That kind of thing always makes me feel unwell.

Nor do I have "something to say" about you. This is a commemoration, not a university lecture. I have a story I want to tell, and given that I have read all your stories it seems only fair that I should be allowed to tell it.

As I was saying, today is January 3, 2019, the fifty-sixth anniversary of the day that one of your number made up her mind that *life is unbearable*.

Let me light a candle. There.

Now for the story:

The night Enayat decided that life was unbearable, she left her son with her mother at 16 Abdel Fattah al-Zeini Street in Dokki and stepped out into the evening with no idea what she was going to do.

For a while, she just walked. She stopped by Misyar's apartment (that is to say, the woman known as Madame al-Nahhas). She seemed calm, her hair cropped so short that Misyar assumed she had come from a salon, and they chatted on the doorstep. She didn't come in. Said she had somewhere to be. She went home and tiptoed up the stairs to her second-floor apartment like a thief. No one was with her when she swallowed the twenty pink pills, so we cannot say for sure just when it was that she fell asleep, her head wedged between two pillows, the blanket smoothed out until it almost hid her from view. Was the balcony window open to the January chill? Did she do what she did by the light of the moon? Was there a lamp by the bed, perhaps, which she switched off as soon as she had settled beneath the blanket?

I know you all love detail. Why, you ask, would a twenty-five-year-old woman with a son who gave her life meaning and a father as tender and enlightened as Abbas al-Zayyat, with a job she loved at the German Archaeological Institute and a second novel under way about a scholar called Keimer, take herself to a hair salon and then come home to kill herself? I have asked the very same thing myself, and often. I have asked her sister and Paula and Misyar, and no one has given me an answer.

As I see it, Enayat never went near a salon. There must be a moment missing from this evening. After leaving her son with her mother, she went back to her apartment and stood in front of the mirror. A moment that no one will understand better than you: the moment in which a woman doesn't know what to do with herself. She doesn't want to go out or talk or write or scream, not even to shatter the mirror which tells her she is there, that she exists.

So on the spur of the moment, Enayat decided to alter her appearance, to bring out the rage and pain inside her, the panic which consumed her, and make it visible to herself: to frame her face in the mirror. She took scissors and hacked at her hair. It was her hair, after all, a part of her identity.

Her visit to Misyar's doorstep with her cropped head was like the soul's last fling, like a woman running headlong having first set herself on fire, like the corpse that grins and urinates as the muscles of its face and bladder relax. She went to Misyar as though sleepwalking, on the brink of reaching out and asking for help. Maybe the sight of her face in the mirror had frightened her. But on Misyar's doorstep she decided that she didn't want any help. She decided that she had somewhere else to be.

Some of you, I would guess, have cut your own hair at least once. Let us think. Our foremother Aisha al-Taymuriyya, who advocated for the hijab till the day she died, would have done so for sure after the death of her daughter Tawhida.

Warda al-Yaziji cropped hers when she heard the rumor that her father and brothers wrote her poems for her.

Malak Hifni Nasif snipped hers away every time her pride brought a fall, like the time the women of the Riyah Bedouin in the Fayoum mocked her for being barren, or when her husband, the Bedouin grandee Abdel Sattar al-Basil, resumed relations with his first wife behind her back, or the time she found out that, after all this, it had been her husband, not her, who was infertile.

May Ziadeh cut it times without number. When her mother died, when she was being treated for insanity at the Asfouriya Asylum, and again when she was discharged and no one came to see her. Bitterest of all, when she realized that she had wasted her life in literary salons with men who called her "beautiful," and that she should have shut herself away instead, and written.

Galila Rida cut it when the doctor informed her that cerebral atrophy meant that her son Galal would be three years old for the rest of his life, or when a Sudanese Arab–nationalist poet publicly humiliated her because she refused to marry him.

Doria Shafik cut hers after the great Taha Hussein shamed her for leading a strike to agitate for the inclusion of women's rights in the revolutionary constitution, describing her and her colleagues as unserious and fame-hungry.

Alifa Rifaat cut hers when she heard them whisper that she promoted lesbianism.

And Latifa al-Zayyat did it too, when she was being torn apart by the double failure of the death of the collectivist dream and her life with the man who had woken the woman in her.

Yet none of you wrote about it. How strange. If you only had. Imagine the anthology we would have—*Shear: A History of Despair*—to be set on the shelf of every library

IMAN MERSAL

alongside Zaynab Fawwaz's great diwan of women's master-
pieces, *Pearls Strewn Through the Women's Quarters*. In addition
to these foundational texts, our anthology could include
writing on your attempts to trace the cuttings of those that
came before you. For example, it could open with a scene
of Aisha al-Taymuriyya standing with scissors in hand, then
one of Warda al-Yaziji and Malak Nasif before their mirrors,
and then May Ziadeh writing about all three. Then May
would write about the cutting of her own hair, to be followed
by Widad Sakakini and Safinaz Kazem and Salma al-Haffar
Kuzbari writing about May cutting her hair, and so on, until
we came to Enayat al-Zayyat.

Let me be clear, though. Inclusion in this anthology is not
going to be predicated on gratitude, like the gratitude that
May Ziadeh felt as she wrote about the women who came
before her (*who opened the way for us*). I would ask everyone
here, conservatives and ideologues and reformists alike, to
respect this fact. This anthology is not going to be a celebra-
tion of our foremothers' achievements, or a matriarchal family
tree sketched out to convey the suffering they endured and
the strength of spirit they required to overcome the terrible
obstacles of their age.

Nor is it to be the preserve of any particular genre. It
is to be a jins jaami, a catch-all for every literary form and
approach. It shall allow mujaanasa, which is to say, coexistence.
The great thirteenth-century dictionary *Lisan al-Arab*, or *The
Tongue of the Arabs*, says the following:

*Jins: meaning "class" or "category," the "genus" of all things and
anything, be it people or birds or parts of speech or prosody or collective*

*nouns. . . . "Jins" is broader in meaning than "type" or "kind,"
and from it is derived "mujaanasa," meaning "to bring together" or
"hybridize," and "tajnees," which means "to make alike."*

Let us make something extraordinary together, something
like the classical Arabic biographies, whose authors would
wander at whim from the subject at hand, digressing as they
pleased. Say a person's name reminds them of a given tribe,
they write about that tribe, then offer a few lines of famous
poetry written in praise of that tribe's great figures before
returning to their main account where they are promptly
reminded of a favorite proverb, so on to the story of how that
proverb came about, and no sooner back on track—back to
the person they should be writing about—than another echo
is touched off, another remembrance, and so on and so on.

All these women here, the precise whens and whys of each
hair-cutting as they stand or sit before their mirrors, is beyond
the reach of my imagination—all of them recognize this
moment, even if they do not tell us so. It is the moment of
confronting the mirror and embodying emptiness, of desiring
to change the self by punishing and disfiguring it, of treating
its features with contempt. Then the moment passes, and the
woman feels the futility of what she has done. Her fury builds.
She falls motionless and enters a phase of monotonous despair,
the phase which the hair requires to grow back.

None of this ever happened to Enayat. Come. Tonight
we celebrate her memory.

23.

Prior to December 13, 2018, all I knew of Isolde was the curt biography that accompanied her article on Keimer:

Isolde Lehnert, MA, born in 1958, studied Egyptology, Near Eastern archaeology, and ethnology in Heidelberg, alongside her work as a graduate librarian. Since 2003, she has been head of the library and archive of the German Archaeological Institute, Cairo. She is currently preparing a biography of Ludwig Keimer.

The day before, on December 12, I had written (in English) to the email address on the website of the German Archaeological Institute, introducing myself and asking them if they had a file on Enayat in the institute's archive. Isolde wrote back to say that the secretary had forwarded her my email, that she was currently in charge of the library, and that the archive was library property. And she added:

At the moment, all I can tell you for sure is that Enayat al-Zayyat did work at the institute's library. The quarterly report, or Vierteljahresbericht, dated 3/31/1963, notes that she died suddenly on January 7 [sic]. The German reads: Die Bibliothekshilfskraft Frau Enayat El-Zayyat verstarb plötzlich am 7. Januar des Jahres.

I can't tell you when she started working here exactly, because the files for 1960 and earlier aren't here. I'll ask at the head office in Berlin to see if they keep personnel files there. The library where she worked was reopened, for the first time since the Second World War, on November 16, 1957, and soon afterwards came into possession of the archive of Ludwig Keimer (1892–1957), which included some ten thousand non-Arabic volumes about Egypt, ancient and modern, approximately 1,200 books in Arabic, and thousands of papers and documents. It took years to catalog and index this extraordinary collection.

I will get back to you when I have new information.

I searched for words to express my gratitude. I wrote that any detail she could provide about Enayat's work with the archive, any pictures of the library in the early 1960s or of the offices where the indexing would have taken place—anything she could imagine—would be of great help.

On December 18, Isolde sent me a series of articles, in German, which had been published in 2007 to commemorate the centennial of the founding of the German Archaeological Institute in Egypt, and she promised to send me photographs and some material in English just as soon as she returned from her Christmas holidays in Germany. And Isolde kept her promise.

Of all the people I had met for Enayat's sake, it was Isolde who took me and my requests most seriously. We both found it extraordinary that Isolde was writing a book about the archive of a man who had also fascinated and inspired a woman whose name she'd never heard before. She started sending me material about the institute and the

Keimer archive, Enayat's registration documents, photographs of the furniture in the room between whose walls Enayat would spend her working day. The institute kept records of everything. It terrified me. The records so comprehensive that if I visited the library, I'd be able to see exactly what Enayat had indexed and cataloged.

The German Archaeological Institute is currently located at 31 Aboul Feda Street in Zamalek, but up until the outbreak of the Second World War it had rented premises on Kamel Mohammed Street, first from a princess of the Alawiyya dynasty, and then from its next owner, a German–Jewish businessman who in 1931 agreed to let them extend their lease. At the start of the war, the British authorities seized the institute's inventory and expelled the German director and staff. When diplomatic relations between Egypt and Germany were restored in the early 1950s, members of staff returned to Cairo to find that the institute's equipment and its library of rare books, which had been established as early as 1897, had been divided up between Alexandria University, King Fouad I University, the Ministry of Antiquities, and various booksellers and antiquarians.

In 1955, Hanns Stock arrived in Cairo with a clear objective: to reestablish the institute in Cairo. He soon found a suitable building in Aboul Feda Street, a villa containing four main dayrooms, six bedrooms, and an office. It was easily large enough for Stock and the staff, and they lived there: Stock and his wife Ines, a financial officer, a secretary, and two assistant archaeologists, Franz Kaiser and Rainer Stadelmann. In 1956, Stock signed a contract with the printers and library content managers, Harrassowitz, to resume printing the institute's periodical after a twelve-year hiatus, and in May the next year he was accredited as director by the main office in Berlin, the official declaration that the institute's work had resumed.

The library had to be reconstituted by any and all means, and Stock had to confront a depressing fact: in October 1956 the library numbered just two hundred and fifty volumes, all of them donations from other institutes. What is more, the books it had lost were incalculably valuable. Their first edition of Richard Lepsius's *Denkmaeler aus Aegypten und Aethiopien* was a twelve-volume work published in 1849, containing around nine hundred illustrations of Ancient Egyptian reliefs and inscriptions, maps and drawings, all with commentary and description, which were for the most part the only surviving record of temples and tombs that had been subsequently destroyed or buried beneath the sands. Since a formal restitution of the library's holdings was out of the question, Stock began to buy them back piecemeal, purchasing institute property whenever he came across it in auction catalogs.

Ludwig Keimer now came into the picture. Unaffiliated and independent, he had been living alone in Egypt since 1928. He was ill, without the means to afford treatment, and he wanted to preserve his own library from oblivion. There were generous offers from the Vatican and the American University in Beirut, as well as others, but Keimer wanted the collection to remain in Egypt. Stock's overtures met with success, and in late May 1957, the institute purchased the contents of Keimer's apartment at 17 Youssef al-Guindy Street in Bab al-Louq, for a flat fee of six thousand Egyptian pounds—which at the time was the equivalent of seventy-two thousand marks—plus a monthly pension for the rest of his life of two hundred pounds. With Keimer's treasure secured, the institute now had an extraordinary library containing thousands of rare folios, periodicals and prints.

Keimer also left them his handwritten notes and a vast collection of photographs and illustrations. Nor were his library's holdings limited to Egyptological works, but included volumes on Near Eastern antiquities, Coptic, Islamic and Arabic culture, rare copies of early European travelogues to Egypt, as well as another collection, equally rare, of scientific treatises on botany, biology, medicine, pharmacology, and anthropology.

In November 1957, in the presence of Minister of Education Kamal al-Din Hussein, an assortment of professors from Cairo University, Minister of State Dr. Georg Anders (who attended as a representative of the Federal Republic of Germany), the German ambassador in Cairo, Walther Becker, and the president of the German Archaeological Institute, Dr. Erich Boehringer, the institute was formally declared reopened. The event received extensive coverage in the Egyptian press, with *al-Ahram* running a long piece about the importance given to archaeology under the leadership of Gamal Abdel Nasser. Keimer was not in attendance: he had passed away on August 16, 1957, just three months after selling his library.

The institute offered to buy the villa and the sale went through on January 7, 1958. The villa was renovated and alterations made, such as the addition of a fourth story containing a living room, seven guest rooms, three bathrooms, a kitchen, and a broad balcony. New laws enacted after the revolution complicated these measures, though things improved with the signing of a treaty of cultural cooperation between Germany and Egypt in 1958. However, the Germans were still in negotiations with UNESCO and the Egyptian government to secure the return of its library and other possessions, or at the very least to gain access to the old catalog that would let them ascertain what had been lost. Their requests were met with silence.

Enayat began work there in 1959, three months after leaving her husband. She had applied before she left him, however, attaching her sister's address to the application to give her space to take the next step. Her husband's refusal to let her work was the straw that broke the camel's back—or perhaps the straw that the drowning woman grasped at only to accompany her under.

She went through a period of training, which included lectures on Keimer and his archive, then the work began. It wasn't particularly exciting at first. Enayat regarded it as a temporary measure, a stop-gap until she had finished *Love and Silence*, until her divorce came through, until she was free to look for something else. She would refer to herself, deprecatingly, as a *shelf botherer*. But by 1961, the unexpected had happened, and she found herself increasingly drawn to

Keimer, his solitude and single-minded dedication to his work. As she worked, she would make notes, jotting down the places he went so that she could visit them herself, or the names of friends so she might look them up; she would spend minutes at a time contemplating a portrait of him or poring over a specimen of his handwriting. And it was at the institute that Enayat met Saad and lost him. It was the institute that had decided to increase her salary by 7 percent, an increase that would have begun at the end of the same January in which she killed herself.

In January 2019, I went to Cairo for nine days after the American University invited me to give a public lecture on the evening of the 19th then attend a conference on the 23rd. My plan was to pay a visit to Madame al-Nahhas on the 17th, meet Isolde and tour the Keimer Archive on the 20th, then go down to Maadi on the 22nd to see the asylum-turned-kindergarten.

The night of the lecture I went out with friends to celebrate and came home to learn that my uncle had died. I would have to travel up to my village in Mansoura early the next morning. On the way down I called Isolde to apologize, and she generously offered to move our meeting to the next day. The very last thing I'd expected during such a short visit was to find myself at a funeral with all my female relatives dressed in black, most of whom I'd not laid eyes on since the last death I'd been here for.

Exhausted and in a dark mood, I presented myself to Isolde.

Isolde clearly loved Keimer. Her eyes shone as she talked about the biography she was writing, about his books and his field notes and his scholarship and journals, about his solitude and his friends. Everything about him seemed to lend meaning to her life and, as we drank coffee in her office, I felt her energy transfer itself to me and my mood clear and lift. Then she took me on a tour of the institute, starting with the third floor, which was once the director's residence but now is used to accommodate visiting researchers. The second floor consists of a large hall and several offices; Isolde's office and the main library are below that, and the rare books collection is housed on the ground floor.

In 1962, the library employed ten members of staff, all of them Germans with the exception of Enayat and one other woman, both of whom had received a German education. That winter, their number swelled to sixteen, when they were joined by specialists who came to oversee their work and conduct research.

We entered the room where Enayat had worked with Hilde and a male colleague. It was rectangular in shape and spacious, with shelves reaching from floor to ceiling on three sides, and a wooden flight of steps which could be moved along the metal rails that fronted each stack. The single balcony looked out over the garden at the rear of the building.

Enayat was here, I thought.

Isolde said, "All the wooden fittings in this room are the work of a carpenter called Ezzat, who installed them before the villa was declared open in 1957. Look how beautiful it is. We've preserved everything just as it was, and we were very lucky to have Ezzat come back in 2005, in his late seventies, to restore the original finishes. We took some pictures of him working and we've kept them in the archive. Sadly, he died two years later."

"Ezzat's workshop used to be at the entrance to the left, just behind the Diwan Bookshop," I told her. What I didn't tell her was that the author Baha Taher had introduced me to Ezzat in 1997 when I'd lived next door to him in Zamalek, and that it was Ezzat who had built my bookshelves with his own hands, shelves that still stand to this day.

Take any two people in this world we live in, however far history and geography have set them apart, and a third lies between them, known to both.

We stood on the balcony, smoking. Isolde told me that she loved working in the building, adored it. She'd been staying on the third floor for six months before she was offered the position in 2003 and had moved out to an apartment of her own. "I studied library science as well as Egyptology," she said: "I worked at Heidelberg University Library for twenty years, but I always assumed that one day I'd do something different. After a difficult period in my life, I decided to make a new start on a different continent. I applied for two jobs, one in New York and the other in Abidjan. Well, I got an acceptance to one of them but they wanted me to give my answer in a day and I panicked. I was in my early forties and I felt like a fool. I might never get another chance! Anyway, a few months later I got an opportunity here and I knew it was for me. I burned my bridges. And I feel I'm lucky to be working on the Keimer Library and to have been here, even during the revolution."

She led me downstairs to the ground floor where the metal storage chests are kept cool and dry all year round and showed me some of the rarer volumes from Keimer's archive: the first Arabic translation of the Gospels; an attempt to decipher hieroglyphics, printed in Paris in 1583; the adventures of Johannes Wild, kidnapped by Turks in 1604 and sold to a Persian merchant who freed him as a gesture of piety during his pilgrimage to Mecca; a manuscript by a Coptic scholar in Rome dated to 1636. The oldest book is an original edition of Hans Tucher's illustrated guide for pilgrims, written following his own pilgrimage to Jerusalem and visits to Cairo and Alexandria. She explained that, dismayed at the size of the library he had been forced to bring with him, Tucher had sought to create a single volume that a traveler could easily transport and this two-kilogram compact guide was the result. First printed in 1482, and so popular that it was to run to six editions in total, it had much in common with a modern guide book: the localities are described in detail and supplemented by useful information concerning preparations for and procedures during the journey.

I could feel Enayat breathing at my shoulder, her shadow brushing past. A shudder ran though me, then I heard Isolde say: "They invited a specialist who analyzes and verifies manuscripts based on their paper, ink, and marginalia. He was able to identify this well-preserved volume as the ninth of only ninety-two copies still in existence. Keimer used to shelve the books that he considered rare and important next to one another, but during the indexing process other rare books were discovered amid the rest of the collection. Between

1959 and 1965 they were gradually identified and relocated from the main library into the air-conditioned archive for protection."

Isolde let me see—no touching—a few pages from Keimer's journal and his drawings, including an example of the entry he would make every time a book came his way: a list of names of everyone who had owned the book before him with the date and other details of his acquisition, plus the shipping number (if it had been posted to him), followed by a description of what he had been doing that day, additional sketches, and then, if any, the book's errata.

This is what Isolde loved in Keimer, and it's likely that this was what Enayat had loved about him, too.

24.

One night in 1933, Ludwig Keimer returned home to his apartment in Bab al-Louq. It had been a long day, locked in a meeting with the committee in charge of drawing up the catalog for the Egyptian Museum which met every Saturday and Monday, followed by dinner at Ghosht, a restaurant in Ezbekiya much patronized by foreigners in Cairo, where he had joined his friend, the ophthalmologist Max Meyerhof.

Enayat wanted to write her version of that night, basing her account on his record of where and when and from whom he'd purchased the Venetian edition of Ibn Sina's *Canon of Medicine*, published in 1562. She had never heard of Max Meyerhof, so she looked him up.

Max Meyerhof had settled in Egypt some thirty years before the night that Enayat was so intent on describing, and that is a story in itself. He had come to Egypt for the first time in 1900, accompanying his cousin Otto Meyerhof, who was hoping to receive relief from kidney pain in the dry air of Helwan. Following the treatment, the cousins visited Aswan and Alexandria, taking with them a set of books authored by their uncle Wilhelm, a professor of Egyptology, who was to die in 1930.

Then they returned to Germany. Otto completed his medical qualifications and would go on to win a Nobel Prize in 1922. A decade later, in flight from the Nazis, he went first to Paris and from there to America. But Max, already a celebrated ophthalmologist at the time of his first trip, had been troubled by the sight of so many Egyptians suffering from eye disease, and in 1903 he returned to the country and opened a clinic for the poor.

He started to study Arabic, and in 1909 was elected president of the Ophthalmological Society of Egypt, going on to become vice-president of both the Institut d'Égypte and the Royal Medical Society. He was visiting Germany when war was declared in 1914, and was unable to return to Egypt until 1922, later opening a clinic in the Immobilia Building where he would charge foreigners high rates and treat the poor for free.

The philosopher Abdel Rahman Badawi recalled that Meyerhof was on excellent terms with socially well-connected and influential intellectuals in Egypt, Sheikh Mustafa Abd al-Raziq in particular. When Meyerhof renounced his German citizenship in 1933, Sheikh Abd al-Raziq helped him become a naturalized Egyptian. He was the author of *From Alexandria to Baghdad*, a study published in 1930, which discusses Greek and Arab medical traditions. Abdel Rahman Badawi appended an Arabic translation of this study to *The Hellenistic Legacy in Islamic Civilization*, which he published in 1940. Meyerhof published extensively about Arab medicine in general, about trachoma in Egypt, and about the history of powdered jequirity as a treatment for eye disease in Egypt.

He was buried in the Jewish cemetery in Old Cairo and his gravestone bore the following inscription in Hebrew: *To the blind he gave light, and his wisdom lit the way for scholars.*

That night in Ghosht, as Keimer and Meyerhof sat drinking a last glass of wine before setting off home, they were accosted by a bookseller who often made the rounds of restaurants frequented by foreigners. The pair were some of his best customers, and he knew them well. Keimer bought a book which weighed 6.2 kg and declared to the pious vendor (who never greeted the German without imploring him to convert to Islam) that with this in his hands he was more than ready to embrace the Faith. The book—the 1562 Venetian edition of *The Canon of Medicine* by Ibn Sina—was to become of all his acquisitions the dearest to his heart. When he got home, Keimer sat down and, as was his custom, recorded his observations: where from and for how much he had bought it, who was with him to witness the transaction, and who had owned it before him, from its genesis in Venice to its appearance on the shelves of Mohammed Ali's physician, Clot Bey, and from there to another doctor, the great Ahmed al-Rashidi, who added his own commentary in the margins, then to the Austrian Hans von Becker, doctor to Khedive Abbas Hilmi II, who had paid ten piastres for it.

Details like these cast a spell over Enayat, who in turn was casting about for some relief from the sense of emptiness, of being cut adrift, that threatened to overwhelm her. She dreamed of writing a book about Keimer's life, and about hers, too. She visited places he had frequented and met with some of his German acquaintances. She discovered, for example, that Howeyati Street, which he had inscribed as his address in Ibn Sina's book, later became 17 Youssef al-Guindy Street, the same address where he lived his entire life in Egypt.

Enayat looked into the friendship which bound Keimer with Meyerhof and a third man, Paul Kraus. From Keimer's notes and journal entries she was able to imagine the times they spent together, and she began to sketch out a map that showed the geography of their Cairo in the thirties and forties, with their home addresses, their places of work, and the locations where they would meet.

She would have learned that Max had donated his library to Paul Kraus in 1936, the same year Kraus arrived in Egypt to take up a job in the Department of Literatures at King Fouad I University, which was also the year that she was born. Paul Kraus lived at 7 Hishmet Pasha Street in Zamalek, and he killed himself in 1944. The library was returned to Max, and when he died the following year all the books went to Keimer.

Enayat must have stopped to think more than once as she was transcribing these scattered fragments from the German's life. Maybe it threw her that the lives of Max and Paul and others were part of the story she was trying to understand. But more than this, it would have been hard for her to look deeply into the life of another person without gazing into her own.

Enayat, it seems, had planned to begin by paying the three men a visit. Or at least this is how I interpreted that strange sentence, whose meaning had eluded me for years: *The journey must begin from the tombs.*

25.

My story with Enayat was over, I assumed. Enayat was a victim no longer. After all, a victim doesn't write; the disaster is described by those who survive it. In my mind, Enayat would continue to write Keimer's story, and that, as it were, was to be my final page.

But multiple endings can sit alongside one another in a single story, as we know.

On April 23, 2019, I was drinking coffee at the Toronto airport, waiting for my flight to Boston and checking my phone, when I saw that I'd received two emails, one from Hani Rashid and the other from Hassan Rashid, both narrating, each from his own point of view, an account of their joint expedition to visit the Rashid family tomb in al-Afifi just two days before.

In the mannered English I had come to expect of him, Hani said that they had met the guard, Hamdan, and that the main burial chambers had needed a new roof, but that they had received a shock on entering the side room in which Enayat was buried. They found her marble headstone broken loose and thrown down while the other graves in the room had been completely destroyed. He wrote that the guard was in the process of clearing the room of its dead so he could live in it, and that he, Hani, intended to go to the archives of the Ministry of Religious Endowments (and to his lawyer) and would use the photographs I had sent to him before to prove the existence of these graves in the room. Hassan's email was brief: a curt note and images of Enayat's headstone lying on the ground. He said that he was on his way home to Oregon, and that he felt upset, but that he would put things right and add Enayat's name to the family tree.

I couldn't think how to reply. It was like a lump in the throat. I looked again at the photograph of the headstone that bore her name, uprooted and cracked across. It would have taken many men and many hammers to break that marble.

Should this be the end of my journey with Enayat: the vandalization of her grave?

Enayat's headstone

Next to me in the airport a little girl was playing with her glasses, making them lift like a plane off the back of her chair and up into the air. Her mother had to keep telling her that they weren't a toy—"Put them on, please"—then minutes later, to ward off boredom, the game would resume.

"Jeanie, I've told you already, they're not a toy. You're going to break them and then you'll be upset. The best way to keep your glasses safe is to keep them on."

"All the time?"

"Yes."

"Even when I'm asleep?"

"Except when you're asleep."

"Then how will I see things in my dreams?"

I glanced up at Jeanie's mother and our eyes met. We laughed in the same instant.

Jeanie had shown more imagination than her tired mother could muster, scorning the Aristotelian logic of the parent, and, with one question, turning it on its head.

Enayat was a unique writer and her imagination out-stripped my ability to trace where she had led. I had promised to visit her every time I returned to Egypt—graves don't move after all—but when I said that I was really making a statement about myself. You will always be a part of my journey, I was telling her. You will be in my steps on the roads of this city which we have loved and hated. You are present in the alienation we both have lived, each in our time. And you are a part of the writing, which has given to us and taken away.

Having first left the German School, Enayat had lost her marriage, then Saad and her son, then life itself. Now she had abandoned her grave. Excised from the official archive, put away in a side room of the family tomb, she knows what she wants. She wants to remain free and weightless, unburdened by personal archive or family tree or marble headstone. For a long time it was me who was walking towards her, but from here on out, it is Enayat who will decide to whom and where she walks.

ENDNOTES

9   *a description of an on-board Babel*: Al-Ayoubi, Ilyas. *A History of Egypt under Khedive Ismail: Volume One (1863–1879)*. Muassasat al-Hindawi, Cairo, 2013. p. 509

10   *to pursue the rout*: Al-Ayoubi, Ilyas. *A History of Egypt under Khedive Ismail: Volume One*. p. 512

10   *The dead were buried in the wadi*: Al-Ayoubi, Ilyas. *A History of Egypt under Khedive Ismail: Volume One*. p. 513

10   *By 1868 he was governor of Cairo*: Al-Rafai, Abd al-Rahman. *The Era of Ismail: Volume Two*. (4th Edition) Dar al-Maaref, Cairo, 1982. p. 111

10   *the precursor of the Ministry of Finance*: Al-Ayoubi, Ilyas. *A History of Egypt under Khedive Ismail: Volume One*. p. 579

10   *Speaker of the final parliamentary sessions*: Al-Rafai, Abd al-Rahman. *The Era of Ismail: Volume Two*. p. 177

11   *among the best classes in society*: Al-Rafai, Abd al-Rahman. *The Era of Ismail: Volume Two*. p. 264

36   *the determining imprint*: Said, Edward W. *Orientalism*. Pantheon Books, New York, 1978. p. 14

42   *the murder of Afghan poet*: Nadia Anjuman (1980–2005) was a poet from Afghanistan. She received her education at an underground school during the Taliban's control of her home province of Herat from 1995 to 2001, and graduated from the Department of Persian Language and Literature at Herat University in 2005, the same year that her first collection, *Gul-e-dodi* [*Dark Flower*] was published. She was expecting the publication of her second collection, *Yek Sabad Delhoreh* [*An Abundance of Anxiety*], when she was murdered by her husband on November 4, 2005. Ajuman became an internationally recognized symbol for the suffering of Afghan women and domestic violence.

48   *Nadia Lutfi was keeper of secrets*: Labib, Foumil. "Nadia Lutfi Reveals the Secret of Enayat al-Zayyat's Suicide," in *al-Musawwar*, May 16, 1967. p. 34

63 *In March 1959, Okasha issued invitations*: Okasha, Tharwat. *My Life in Politics and Culture: A Memoir*. (3rd Edition) Dar al-Shurouq, Cairo, 2000. p. 414

63 *immediately drew up plans to build*: Okasha, Tharwat. *My Life in Politics and Culture: A Memoir*. p. 429

65 *Anxiety, come, enfold me*: This extract from Enayat's journal was published in 1967 alongside Foumil Labib's interview with Nadia Lutfi. The same passage also appears in the pages from Enayat's journal which I acquired from Nadia Lutfi in July 2015.

73 *a film had been made*: *Love and Silence* (1973), a film by Nahdat Misr Productions (Wali al-Sayed). Director: Abdel Rahman Sharif. Screenwriter: Masoud Ahmed. Cast: Nelly, Ahmed Abdel Halim, Nour al-Sharif, Madiha Hamdi, Ashraf Abdel Ghafour.

80 *And the red doll*: Shah, Hosn. "I Shall Never Die: The Journal of Enayat al-Zayyat," in *Akher Saa'a*, May 24, 1967

  The passage quoted here is one of six paragraphs, each given a title by Shah, taken from Enayat's journals.

82 *the complete personal archive*: McKemmish, Sue. "Evidence of Me," in *The Australian Library Journal* 45:3, 1996. pp. 174–87

86 *recordings of the serialization*: *Love and Silence* (1973), a radio serial broadcast on the General Program. Writer: Azza al-Sherbini. Director: Hussein Othman. Cast: Mahmoud Morsi, Salah al-Saadani, Farouq Naguib, Farouq Suleiman, Nadia Shinawi. Recording and editing: Qutb Mohammed, Ali Hamid, Mustafa Abdel Halim.

  Enayat's name is mentioned during the opening sequence of each episode, but a search through the archives of the Television and Radio Union reveals that it was excluded from the reference card attached to these broadcasts.

97 *"a cup of milk for every child"*: Haggag, Hanan. "The Tin Cup of Milk that Turned to Scrap," in *al-Ahram*, Issue 46563, May 5, 2014

99 *something about the Mesaha School*: Al-Ayoubi, Ilyas. *A History of Egypt under Khedive Ismail: Volume One*. p. 178

99 *writes about the two commissioners*: Al-Ayoubi, Ilyas. *A History of Egypt under Khedive Ismail: Volume One*. p. 793

123 *I have tried to tell a truth*: Al-Sayyid, Esam. "Recently Honored at the National Festival of Cinema, Hosn Shah Speaks Out: I Was the Reason the Personal Status Laws Were Changed," in *al-Hayat* (London), December 2, 2010

125 *carries the text of Law 25*: *Egyptian Affairs*, Issue 27, March 25, 1929. pp. 2–7

127 *campaigning against Law 25 for over a decade*: Personal Status Law 25, 1929, was not abolished in response to *I Want a Solution*; all Sadat did was enact Law 44, 1979, which meant that a house of obedience ruling no longer had compulsory force. However, if a wife did not return to the house of obedience, then she was considered insubordinate and no longer entitled to material rights such as financial support. In other words, the only beneficiaries of this law were women who were financially secure enough to waive these rights. Subsequently, even these limited reforms were challenged before the Constitutional Court and Law 100, 1985, was issued in order to avoid what was termed their "constitutional flaws."

128 *Enayat's younger sister, Azima al-Zayyat*: Shah, Hosn. "What Does the Personal Status Law Want? Enayat al-Zayyat's Tragedy Reprised," in *Akher Saa'a*, Issue 1699, May 17, 1967. pp. 20–1

129 *But who is Azima al-Zayyat?*: Shah, Hosn. "What Does the Personal Status Law Want? Enayat al-Zayyat's Tragedy Reprised"

131 *In her submission, the plaintiff states*: I obtained copies of Enayat al-Zayyat's case files before the various courts on condition that I not reveal my source.

132 *She entered a marriage without love*: Shah, Hosn. "I Shall Never Die: The Journal of Enayat al-Zayyat," in *Akher Saa'a*
     Shah entitled this paragraph "The key of deliverance."

136 *Nothing can frighten me now*: Shah, Hosn. "I Shall Never Die: The Journal of Enayat al-Zayyat," in *Akher Saa'a*
     Shah added lines from an earlier journal entry (written in 1961) to this passage and entitled both "I am existence."

145 *Giants of Egyptology*: Lehnert, Isolde. "Giants of Egyptology: Ludwig Keimer," in *KMT* 23:1, 2012. pp. 74–7

169 *A serious fire had destroyed*: Mayers, Marilyn A. *A Century of Psychiatry: The Egyptian Mental Hospitals*, a doctoral dissertation for Princeton University, 1984, published by University Microfilms International, Ann Arbor, 1987. p. 56

170 *accommodated in the stable block next door*: Mayers, Marilyn A. *A Century of Psychiatry: The Egyptian Mental Hospitals*. pp. 91–2

171 *the opportunity to learn basic crafts and trades*: Mayers, Marilyn A. *A Century of Psychiatry: The Egyptian Mental Hospitals*. p. 93

171 *from 465 to 2,472 over the same period*: Mayers, Marilyn A. *A Century of Psychiatry: The Egyptian Mental Hospitals*. p. 101

171 *the principal cause was said to be sex*: "Annual Report of Council, and Balance Sheet for the Year 1904," in *Brain: A Journal of Neurology*, Volume 28, 1905

175 *Wretched beauty: death's silent field*: Among Nadia Lutfi's collection of Enayat al-Zayyat's papers is this document, dated September 23, 1962.

193 *a passionate advocate of Arab causes*: Sidqi, Jadhibiyah. *America and Me*. (1st Edition) Maktabat al-Nahda al-Misriya, Cairo, 1962

193 *a published author in her own right*: See:
Kazem, Safinaz. "Jadhibiya Sidqi Is a High-Born Writer Whose Stories Blaze with Passion and Who Prays the Full Five Times a Day," in *al-Jeel*, Issue 383, April 27, 1959. pp. 1–19

In this interview, Sidqi presents a comprehensive portrait of a writer who is daring at her desk and conservative in real life. At one point, when Kazem asks her about the intensity of love in her writing, Sidqi says, "I write about it as I picture it—stormy, powerful—and I live through my articulation of this emotion."

199 *"Taha Fawzi, who translated from the Spanish"*: I found nothing definite on Taha Fawzi. A translator from Italian by the same name was active between 1947 and 1976, his translations including *Cuore* by Edmondo De Amicis (1957), Gabriele D'Annunzio's *L'innocente*, and selections from Dante (1965).

205 *I want my feet to feel new ground*: Shah, Hosn. "I Shall Never Die: The Journal of Enayat al-Zayyat," in *Akher Saa'a*

Interestingly, the dream of escaping and traveling to a land far away as depicted here is also present in *Love and Silence*.

209 *On April 21, 1967*: Al-Alem, Mahmoud Amin. "She Died Even as She Triumphed," in *al-Musawwar*, Issue 2219, April 21, 1967. This article was republished in his later book (*Forty Years of Applied Criticism: Structure and Semantics in the Contemporary Arab Novel and Short Story*. (1st Edition) Dar al-Mustaqbal al-Arabi, Cairo, 1994. pp. 456–8) but without mentioning its previous publication in *al-Musawwar*.

211 *Silence is a stone*: Al-Zayyat, Latifa. "She Died and Died Not," in *al-Hiwar*, December 2, 1967

212 *He was the first man to wake the woman in me*: Al-Zayyat, Latifa. *The Search: Personal Papers*. Kitab al-Hilal, No. 502, Cairo, October 1992. p. 71

213 *According to his own account*: Al-Alem, Mahmoud Amin. *Testimonies and Perspectives: Volume Five of the History of the Communist Movement in Egypt*. (1st Edition) The Center for Arab and African Studies in cooperation with the Committee for Documenting the Pre-1965 History of the Egyptian Communist Movement, Cairo. pp. 147–74

213 *in 1963, al-Qawmiyya Publishing was merged*: Okasha, Tharwat. *My Life in Politics and Culture: A Memoir.* p. 720

214 *placing it under Mahmoud Amin al-Alem's direction*: Okasha, Tharwat. *My Life in Politics and Culture: A Memoir.* pp. 722–3

224 *I don't mean a thing to anybody*: Labib, Foumil. "Nadia Lutfi Reveals the Secret of Enayat al-Zayyat's Suicide," in *al-Musawwar.* p. 34

227 *don't transcribe all the necessary data in subsequent editions*: As with Dar al-Shurouq editions of Naguib Mahfouz's novels, the publisher makes no reference to the dates or publishers of previous editions.

228 *that Arab women writers were primarily concerned with nationalism*: Shaaban, Bothaina. *Voices Revealed: Arab Women Novelists 1898–2000.* (2nd Edition) Dar al-Adaab, Beirut, 2002. p. 18

228 *the standard misapprehension*: See, for example:

Bakr, Salwa. "Enayat al-Zayyat: Her Love and Her Silence," for *al-Badil*, republished by copts-united.com on March 9, 2009

Abou al-Naga, Shereen. "She Died Even as She Triumphed," in *al-Hayat* (London), January 2015

229 *entitled "The Unknown Author Died"*: Mansour, Anis. "The Unknown Author Died," in *al-Musawwar*, July 23, 1963

238 *The usual—indeed, the clichéd—way of describing empathy*: Young-Bruehl, Elisabeth. *Subject to Biography: Psychoanalysis, Feminism, and Writing Women's Lives.* Harvard University Press, Cambridge, 2000. p. 22

243 *What do my critics know*: Al-Masry, Hussein Muguib. *Links Between the Arabs, the Persians, and the Turks.* (1st Edition) Dar al-Thaqafa, Cairo, 2001. pp. 268–9

244 *what Mervat Hatem wrote about Aisha*: Hatem, Mervat F. *Literature, Gender, and Nation-Building in Nineteenth-Century Egypt: The Life and Works of Aisha Taymur.* Palgrave Macmillan, New York, 2013

249 *who opened the way for us*: Ziadeh, May. *Warda al-Yaziji.* Al-Hindawi, Cairo, 2012. p. 7

260 *Between 1959 and 1965*: The information in this chapter draws on my private conversations with Isolde Lehnert and the following articles:

Kehrer, Nicole. "100 Jahre am Nil. Die Geschichte des Deutschen Archäologischen Instituts in Kairo" in Dreyer, Günter and Polz, Daniel (eds), *Begegnung mit der Vergangenheit. 100 Jahre in Ägypten*, Mainz, 2007. pp. 3–15

Lehnert, Isolde. "Was Bücher erzählen. Die Bibliothek des Instituts und die Schätze des Ludwig Keimers," in *Begegnung mit der Vergangenheit. 100 Jahre in Ägypten.* pp. 16–24

264 *which he published in 1940*: Badawi, Abdel Rahman. *The Hellenistic*

Legacy in Islamic Civilization. (1st Edition) Maktabat al-Nahda al-Misriya, Cairo, 1940. pp. 37–100

264 *Meyerhof published extensively about Arab medicine*: For more on Meyerhof, see:

Badawi, Abdel Rahman. *The Encyclopedia of Orientalists*. (3rd Edition) Dar al-Ilm lil Millayeen, Beirut, 1993. pp. 540–3

265 *To the blind he gave light*: Badawi, Abdel Rahman. *The Encyclopedia of Orientalists*. p. 542

IMAN MERSAL is an Egyptian poet, essayist, translator, and literary scholar. Currently professor of Arabic language and literature at the University of Alberta, Canada, she is the author of five books of Arabic poetry, selections from which have been translated into numerous languages. *The Threshold*, translated into English by Robyn Creswell, was published by Farrar, Straus and Giroux in 2022, and was shortlisted for the 2023 Griffin Poetry Prize and won the 2023 National Translation Award in Poetry. She is the recipient of the 2021 Sheikh Zayed Book Award in Literature for *Traces of Enayat*.

ROBIN MOGER is a translator of Arabic living in Barcelona. He has translated poetry and prose, including Haytham El Wardany's *The Book of Sleep* and Mohamed Kheir's *Slipping*.